Confessions of a

Freelance Translator

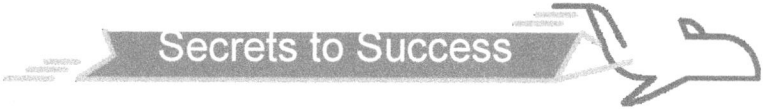

Secrets to Success

Confessions of a Freelance Translator:

Secrets to Success

Gary Smith

2016

First Printing: 2016

Second Printing: 2017

ISBN 978-84-608-6565-0

@GaryGlokalize

info@glokalize.com

Cover design: Judith Vargas Álvarez

https://judithdesigner.com/

<u>Dedication</u>

This book is dedicated to:

My friends, colleagues and constructive critics around the world for their invaluable advice and support.

Erik Hansson for creating and hosting the Facebook group *Things Translators Never Say* that inspired the name and corresponding section of this book.

Content

Who is this book for?

This book is for aspiring[1] and working translators who wish to earn a successful living as a translator.

By *successful*, I mean somebody who makes at least a comfortable living doing a professional, full-time job, not somebody who translates as a hobby or 24/7 including weekends to meet unreasonable deadlines for a miserly income.

By *translator*, I do not mean someone who speaks two or more languages well. I mean a well-read person with impeccable grammar who to all intents and purposes is bilingual, whether a mother-tongue speaker or not, and who has a deep understanding not only of the languages but also the cultures that use them, including a mastery of different registers (it is not the same to translate a tabloid as to translate the "serious" press). Mario Vargas Llosa once said that to be a good writer one must first be a good reader. This is also true of translators.

If this describes you or who you would like to be, whether you are currently qualified, experienced and working as a translator or would like to be, then this book is for you.

Welcome to one of the best jobs in the world.

----

[1] For those starting out in freelance translation, see the section *Starting Out*.

Why become a freelance translator?

The obvious reason that comes to mind is the first syllable in the word *freelance* itself. You are free to decide when and where to work, within limits. Those limits are set by your clients in agreement with you, and thus the level of freedom you have will depend largely on the clients you have and your relationship with them. Get it right and you will have more freedom in terms of both your time and money. Get it wrong and you may as well forget that first syllable, since you may end up working long, unsociable hours for little pay.

So let's look at how to get it right.

Client Relations: The Basics

The perfect client

Everyone has their own idea of the perfect client. It may be the one that pays the best fee, the one that gives you relatively easy or enjoyable jobs or the one that simply treats you well.

As an example, I was once on my way to a congress and was killing time at an airport during a stopover for a couple of hours when a client called me with an urgent job. As usual when I'm at a congress, I had notified all my regular clients in good time that I would be away and unavailable, leaving them with a few email addresses of trusted colleagues. However, this client insisted that they wanted *me* to do the job. I explained the situation, that I was in an airport with no Wi-Fi and not exactly the best working conditions. Even so, they insisted that I do the job, finally extending the deadline until I could connect to the Wi-Fi at my hotel and send the work that night. I applied my urgent fee and grudgingly accepted, not wanting to upset a good, long-term client.

That night after delivering the job, I reflected on whether or not this was the kind of client I wanted. As a freelance worker, one has to find a good life/work balance so I didn't like the idea of this client insisting on my working under such conditions when they knew I wasn't really available. However, they were frankly nice people, they knew this situation was an exception and the work was interesting and for a good cause. Then I realised that this client had just shown me that they were willing to go out of their way to give me the job, practically begging to give me their money. It suddenly struck me that this is exactly the kind of client everybody is aiming for. So I guess I'd made it. One of this book's aims to give advice about how to attain such loyalty in clients.

In order to find and keep such clients, we must first put ourselves in their shoes to understand what they are looking for in a translator. And in order to do *that*, we are going to look at examples of many different professions that we all know well and have experienced in our daily lives, because translation, whether we like it or not, is affected by simple market psychology and the rules of supply and demand as in any other profession where there are buyers and sellers. Throughout this book, I shall be giving simple examples of the relationship between client and service-provider that we can all relate to, then applying them to the world of freelance translation.

<u>How do potential clients see you?</u>

First, let's put ourselves in our potential client's shoes. The monolingual, monocultural client needs a text translated but knows nothing about translation, how to find a good translator, or how much they may reasonably charge. Their idea of a human translator may be a studious hermit sitting at a desk piled with paper dictionaries, holding a quill poised in the air as they muse over a mixed metaphor. On the other hand, the only translator everybody in the developed world has heard of is Google Translate. Everybody has used the famous word cruncher once in a while to see what their Chinese tattoo actually means or get the gist of a foreign news article or recipe. So our potential client knows of Google Translate at least. They also know it is capable of translating thousands of words per second for free. And then they turn to you and discover that it will take days and cost several hundreds or thousands of euros. Understandably, they may well be taken aback.

To understand their predicament, imagine your car breaks down in a town you don't know and you have to find a decent mechanic to repair it. At one garage they nonchalantly tell you it's going to cost €50 and take half an hour. At another, they shake their heads sagely and tell you it'll cost €1,000 and take a week. Who's telling the truth? Who knows what they're doing? Who's trying to rip you off? In order to gain a potential client's confidence, there are little strategies that mechanics can and do use to allay our fears and convince us to choose their services. We, too, can apply such strategies to gain our clients' trust. We shall look at them throughout this book.

The car mechanic, like the translator, the dentist, the lawyer, or even the hairdresser, is one of those professions with its jargon and the average customer's lack of knowledge that leads you to fear that the service-provider may be trying to trick you into paying more or giving you services you don't really need or want. Such professionals, like translators, have to overcome this fear at first if we are going to gain a new or potential customer's trust. On the other hand, when we *do* gain a customer's trust, it is often a long-term one, precisely because they are reluctant to try out another, unknown professional. Better the "devil", service provider or translator they already know.

<u>The consultant</u>

Here's another typical customer/service-provider relationship we all know: the clothes shop. What, you may ask, does a clothes shop have in common with a translator? The answer: there are lots of them to choose from, so you have to do something to make your services and products noticeable and worth repeating.

Ask yourself this question: If you buy some clothes that don't really suit you, whose fault is it—yours or the shop's?

Nobody forced you to buy those clothes, though the shop assistant may have used some charming sales talk. Or maybe you didn't even talk to the shop assistant but thought you knew exactly what you wanted. This is a common mistake we all make—believing that we know more about fashion and what looks good on us than the professionals who work with clothes for a living. Our clients can make a similar mistake when checking our translations by themselves, assuming they have a good enough grasp of the language to meddle with it.

Indeed, a common mistake we all make as customers is assuming we know what is best for us instead of listening to and trusting the professionals (in this case, fashion and textiles professionals). But one thing that sets expensive, boutique clothes shops apart from the big, cheap chain stores is precisely the professional, personalised advice and attention their trained, experienced staff can give us.

Many shop assistants work by commission, however, and will be glad to sell you anything and take your money. Nevertheless, if those clothes end up at the back of your wardrobe never to be worn, you probably won't feel like going back to that shop in a hurry, unless it is to change the clothes if possible. In other words, for the sake of some sharp sales talk and a quick sale, the shop may have lost an unsatisfied customer's trust for life.

As an example, a friend of mine once had her eye on a white bikini and when the summer sales began she went straight to the shop to buy it. However, she ended up walking out of that shop with a multi-coloured swimsuit. What had happened in that shop to make her change her mind?

"Did they talk you into buying a more expensive garment?" I asked her. No; in fact my friend was extremely satisfied with her similarly-priced purchase and wore it all summer. Even so, why had the shop even bothered to persuade my friend to buy the coloured swimsuit if she was already going to buy a garment anyhow? The answer: because they realised what the customer actually *needed*, not what she *thought* she needed. The shop assistant is the professional when it comes to clothes and fashion, not my friend. A good clothes shop will not just sell you clothes, but give you expert advice. If you walk out of the shop with clothes that don't suit you, *it is not your fault but the shop's*.

Here's another question: Why do we go to clothes shops in the first place? To buy clothes? Well, no; I'm sure we all have enough clothes to meet the essential purpose of covering and protecting our bodies, so we actually go to clothes shops with another purpose in mind: to improve our image. Maybe we have a wedding coming up, a job interview, a translators' congress (!) or we simply feel the need to move with the times so as not to look outdated. So, we usually go shopping for clothes to look good (even for sports or work our image is still a factor). If that is the case, what kind of shop are we going to prefer: one that lets us buy whatever takes our fancy, or one that tells us what's in fashion, what tones go with our complexion and what styles go with our different body shapes and sizes? Obviously, even if we don't always buy garments at that shop, out of all of the shops in the mall we will always go back to the one that gives us good advice. A good clothes shop where we will always return doesn't just sell us clothes; they become our fashion consultants to whom we listen in order to improve our image. Of course, this has to be done with tact. Nobody likes being told they have bad taste in clothes, especially ladies like my friend! (In fact, the sales assistant gave her the white bikini to try on and merely handed her the other garment to compare, knowing that my friend would see the difference for herself and make the right choice.)

Likewise, just as a good clothes shop does not merely sell clothes, translators do not merely sell texts. A good, trustworthy translator also gives their clients sound cultural and linguistic advice. People go to clothes shops not merely to buy clothes, but essentially to improve their image. Similarly, we need to understand what our translation client actually needs; what their ulterior motive is. A lawyer may need to understand the context of a contract in another country's legal system; a scientist or engineer may need to "sell" their research or patent in another culture; or a marketing department may need to sell their product to very different target consumers from different cultural backgrounds, age groups or social circles. This is one way we can begin to gain our clients' trust: by showing that we do not merely translate texts, but can also give them expert advice. It is also a chance to show them your knowledge and what you can do for them, possibly even suggesting other services they hadn't considered beforehand. (Studies show it is much easier to sell additional, related services to a customer who has already bought one, having opened up their mind to the idea of buying in general.)

What's the difference between a tailor and a cheap chain clothes store? Obviously, the first difference that springs to mind is that the former is more expensive. But why? Because they supposedly produce a better quality product and service, of course. This is clearly noticeable in the end product but also in carrying out the service. A tailor takes your measurements, studies your requirements, asks you questions about your tastes and needs, and listens to your answers. Literally, they *tailor* the product to the client, giving a professional, bespoke service that generates loyalty in their customers. You can do the same with most other services, including translation. We shall look at how to do so in this book.

Don't forget that you can also find new clients by tactfully pointing out their badly translated websites, brochures, etc. and leaving them your contact information. This is much more positive and practical than simply moaning about them in a translators' forum or elsewhere. (Indeed, you should avoid complaining about companies' texts publicly, since your potential clients may see your complaints and become wary of working with you.)

The thing that most sets us apart from Google Translate is our human understanding of the contexts, the subtle ironies and cultural pitfalls. There are puns, jokes, metaphors or simply ideas out of the blue that only a human with a good understanding of the cultures involved can grasp and use or avoid when necessary. It is people who read the final texts, not machines. We are not only a bridge between languages, but also between cultures. We should therefore aim to be our clients' linguistic and cultural consultants to whom they may turn whenever they need such advice.

Giving advice such as telling a Spanish hotel to change their meal times to suit British tourists *costs us nothing*, yet can be *priceless to our clients* and ensure their loyalty. By doing so, they will keep coming back and never forget us when they need to translate a text.

<u>"Are you available?"</u>

So how does your potential monolingual client find you? In the Yellow Pages? Probably not, unless it's an elderly individual with no internet connection, for example, or the Yellow Pages website. Again, let's put ourselves in the client's shoes with another everyday example. When you're in a city you don't know and you want to find a good restaurant amid all those restaurants you can see on the street, what are the clues you look out for?

One of the most obvious clues is to see which restaurants are packed with local diners. Clearly, local people know where the good restaurants are, so all we have to do is to see where they go and follow them. On the other hand, if you see a completely empty restaurant, what kind of impression does that give you? The first question that springs to mind is "Why is it empty?" This is important to bear in mind when letting your clients know your availability. If you say "yes" to all job offers (even on a Friday evening, with a lower fee, etc.) then you are effectively saying that you are desperate for work. As soon as the client is aware of this, they are obviously in a strong position to negotiate fees and tight deadlines with you. If you're not desperate for work, make sure you know where to put your limits and stand your ground. Have a fairly clear idea beforehand of what your minimum fee is, what your urgency fee is (for weekend or rush jobs, for example), etc. The danger of not doing so is that you may become the client or agency's dogsbody, the one to whom they always send work at the weekend or urgently; the one who will accept low fees; the one who takes no holidays.

I have a translator friend who works for the same agency as myself (though he doesn't know this!). He sometimes boasts to me of how he is the agency's "fix-it-man", the one they can always turn to when they need an urgent job doing, be it at the weekend or at no extra cost. Little does he know that the same agency tends to send me work on Mondays and Tuesdays, leaving the weekend jobs to him because they know he always accepts them!

Provided you are not desperate for work, the client needs to be aware that you are capable of rejecting work if you wish to have a firm position to negotiate good terms for your work. Of course, if it is a good, regular client, you may agree to do one-off rush jobs once in a while to keep them happy, but make sure they know this is an exception for a special client.

It is also important for end clients to learn that good, professional translation takes time. One way to teach them this is the urgent fee, an extra percentage on top of your usual fee for rush jobs.

Saying "yes" to all jobs can also give the impression that you are not very professional. Do you really have time to do the job properly? Is it a field you specialise in? Can you find reliable colleagues to form a team for a big project, maintaining coherent, consistent terminology, all before the deadline?

When the client knows you are a good translator but not always available, a common sales factor that I call the "window of opportunity" comes into play. You've probably noticed how big companies often play on the potential customers' sense of urgency with such expressions as "while stocks last". Of course, no stocks are infinite, so anything they sell will always be "while stocks last", but the simple phrase reminds potential customers that the product *will not always be available*, so they'd better buy it while it is.

Limited availability can also be a sign of quality. There is a restaurant in Catalonia that was known as the world's best restaurant for a couple of years. Unfortunately, precisely because of this it had a waiting list of at least six months. Can you imagine phoning that restaurant on a Friday evening and asking for a table for twenty people? Obviously, you wouldn't be surprised to hear them say "no". You would not think they are unreliable or unprofessional for rejecting your offer, either. On the contrary, you would realise that it must be a good restaurant and remember to book earlier next time.

At the other end of the scale, if you've ever been to rather seedy tourist resorts or landmark areas, you may have seen some waiters standing outside trying to convince passers-by to come into their restaurants. However, you'll also see if you look carefully that the successful restaurants don't need to do this. Indeed, I find those waiters trying to entice people inside their restaurants to be quite annoying. The same thing often happens with many of the unsolicited CVs I receive.

So, what happens when you don't have a lot of work but you don't want to appear desperate? How do you let your clients know about your availability without begging for work or annoying them?

The trick here is how and when to tell them you're available. Try to give a reason other than just telling them why they should look at your CV and how great it would be for them if you translate their texts. If it's a past client, maybe you can send them an email to inform them that you've just received the last payment from them in your bank account, for example. ("Oh, and by the way, I'm available again now.") Or perhaps there's a tax matter or email address change they should know about. Another good time is when you have just got back from a holiday, congress or business trip. You should ideally warn your clients that you are going to be away beforehand, but you can also send this availability reminder as a circular to all of the clients and agencies you have ever worked with. Some of them may have forgotten all about you after a few years, so this will act as a reminder.

Mentioning congresses and seminars etc. is always good as it reminds them that you are still very much in the translation business and taking it seriously.

<u>Vacations</u>

As for holiday periods, in some countries most people usually go on holiday at about the same time of year, so this is a good time to find work from agencies whose regular translators are not going to be available. In Mediterranean Europe, for example, many people go on holiday almost throughout August. If you send your CV to agencies in the last week of July to tell them you'll be available over the holiday period, you may get lucky and take on work that their regular translators are not available for. Then there are national holidays in all countries. You might like to write to Brazilian agencies a week before the carnival begins (or just afterwards, when their translators may have hangovers!), or to agencies in the USA a few days before 4th July or Thanksgiving. Check out national holidays in the countries whose languages you translate from; you can find them easily in Wikipedia, for example.

And don't forget that you also need a vacation yourself some time, too!

Goodwill gestures

Don't forget relevant holiday greetings such as Christmas, either. If you have a loyal client you like doing business with, send them a card or even a small, relevant present as a token of your gratitude and goodwill. It's much more difficult to stop working with such a friendly translator, or to get involved in disputes over work.

You could also follow your clients' companies in the social networks to show your loyalty and likewise include them in any regular newsletters or blog updates you may have yourself (not too often; you don't want to spam them; once a month is fine).

Smile—it's free!

I have a friend who worked as a salesperson in a big multinational for years who I have observed when she asks people for favours. We may be at a restaurant, for example, and she will ask the waiter for something a little extra with a beaming smile on her face. She usually gets her way, even if she has to calmly insist, but her smile and good manners never disappear. It has been proven that when we smile this also has an effect on our own attitude, actually making us genuinely a little happier ourselves. There's no faking that! Remember that people really can "hear" your smile on the phone, too. Record your own voice and hear it for yourself. In fact, we should all practice our phone voice and elevator speech by listening to ourselves, as we don't know what we sound like ourselves.

Types of client and how to deal with them

The hesitant client

Clients who are unsure of whether or not to hire your services need reassurance. Give them facts, data and some words about your experience.

The demanding client

For demanding clients, mimic their own demanding style, which will reassure them. For example, if they like to use the phone a lot to confirm how the job is going etc., phone them too when the job is done, asking if they've received it, telling them a little about what you did, etc.

The loyal client

With your regular customers, get on first name terms, tell them little anecdotes about your life and ask about theirs (nothing too personal) and maybe give them little snippets of information that are irrelevant but harmless. If you know they support a football team, you could mention the latest result, for example. This is common decency and friendliness, but sometimes when working we can forget how little details like this make our clients' working lives more pleasant.

The hurried client

Once in a while, even the best of clients may be in an unavoidable hurry. Mirror their sense of urgency with comments such as "I'll get on it as soon as I can / right away".

The aggressive client

If we decide to continue working with an aggressive or even rude client, we should let such people "let off steam". If it's a phone call, for example, don't interrupt. Indeed, agree with them where you actually do, so that they can see you're not being unreasonable. When they have finally gone through their tirade and have nothing left to say, you may now enter the conversation calmly and give your point of view or explanation. *Do not* mirror their aggression.

The haggler

Serious, professional service providers such as translators don't haggle over their fees. While your fee for a particular job may change due to extra services and the reasons given below in the section *"How much do you charge?"*, we should leave haggling for the backstreet bazaar or the poker game. If they'd like to know the reasons for your fee that they consider high, have an answer ready describing the services and quality you provide if you like.

Phone conversation strategies

Another phone tip to remember is to avoid beginning your sentences with a negative. When I was a small child, my parents nicknamed me "Yeah-but" because whenever they denied me something I would begin my retort with "Yeah, but…" It actually works. Begin your reply with the word "yes" and acknowledge your interlocutor's argument before continuing to explain your point of view and destroying their case if necessary. As translators and writers, I am sure you are all well aware of the usefulness of structuring arguments in this way: present and acknowledge the opposing arguments first, then knock them down and present yours, followed by a resounding conclusion.

Taking this a step further, it's even better to take out the "but" and replace it with "and", thereby indicating that what follows is as positive as the opening. So instead of saying, "Your text is very interesting, *but* it can be improved," you can say, "Your text is very interesting *and* it can be improved to be even better [by spelling the words correctly and putting them in the correct order to make coherent sentences. ☺]."

Similarly, there is the "sandwich criticism" technique, which may be useful when clients ask for an unwarranted discount, for example. This involves 'sandwiching' the bad news between two pieces of good news. For example:

"That last text you sent me was very interesting. In fact, I enjoy working on the texts you usually send me. / However, I'm afraid I can't possibly bring the fee down; it's already low for me. / Before I forget, thanks for the last timely payment and professional project management. I like working with you guys."

If you are cold-called with a job offer from a fairly condescending individual, it is always useful to ask questions yourself, too. Never forget that as a freelancer, your relationship with clients and agencies should be as equals in a business transaction, not as a boss and their employee. By asking simple questions like "To whom am I speaking?", "Where are you based?", "Can you tell me a little bit about your company, or where I can find your website?" etc., you can turn the psychological tables on a haughty caller and earn their respect. It is important from the outset that your clients realise you are an equal in the process if you want them to listen to you later on in the translation process or when negotiating fees. Your client is not your boss.

If you should get an irate, dissatisfied customer (who may well be completely wrong but insistent), on the phone, I repeat that before you reply it's essential to let them "let off steam" by listening to them until they have nothing more to say. Only then will they be psychologically ready to listen to you. And remember to show you agree with them where you actually do, to show you're not being unfair (e.g. "Yes, I can see the final text isn't what you wanted" [but it's your internal proofreader's fault]).

And again, never forget that it's very difficult to say "no" to someone who's smiling at you. In any case, it's plainly nicer to create a positive working atmosphere with your clients for your own good. We all like to work with pleasant people. You'll all feel better for it and communication between you will go more smoothly.

<u>Closing the sale</u>

If you come across the hesitant client mentioned above, use language that implies the sale is a foregone conclusion. For example, if they ask vague, conditional questions about when you would deliver the text if they finally give you the job, reply with more direct language like "I'll send it to you next Tuesday by 11 a.m., OK?"

You can also close the sale with such clients by giving them two options, thereby psychologically giving them a freedom of choice, but where both options involve a sale. In the example just mentioned, for instance, you could give them two fees and deadlines, one urgent and one "ordinary". You could even make one of the options much less likely to be chosen, but the fact that you let the client choose helps them feel more at ease with you. Remember that salespeople are not called "show people", because their job is not simply to *show* the product or service on offer, but to *sell* it. That is your job, too. Don't be shy about it; your livelihood may depend on it.

And if you're not available…?

Nearly all translators at some point will have too little work or too much. Unless your projects are usually quite long texts such as book translations, you will spend much of your time trying to get the balance right.

Don't forget that you may decide to reject a job not only due to a lack of availability, but because it simply isn't a specialisation of yours. In this case, so as to keep the client within your circles, you may have a reliable colleague who can do the job and is available. Try this before rejecting the job, but remember to tell your colleague to use your fee (or raise it if it is a specialised text) so as not to undercut you or even take the client from you.

Should I outsource?

With growing success and periods of too much work, at some point all translators end up asking themselves if they should become an outsourcer. You should avoid outsourcing work from agencies (at least not without telling them), as this will bring down the end translator's fee (you will want a commission for handling the project) and put upward pressure on the price charged to the end client (the agency will have to make up for your higher fees). You may even decide it may be worth starting up an agency yourself.

There are some obvious considerations to take into account before outsourcing. Firstly, it does not mean simply collecting a finder's fee for the work you outsource. You need to organise communication with the client, deal with possible problems in the source and target texts, and obviously find the right people to revise (check the target text against the source text, looking for mistranslations or missing information), proofread (check the target text alone for grammar, spelling etc.) and review the text (check it for style, suitability to the target readers etc.)[2].

All of this clearly takes up your time. Worse still, if you outsource to unsuitable translators, you may find yourself doing much more work because you have to re-do the translation. This implies a loss of income for you in terms of pay per hour.

---

[2] Note that the translator should also do these anyway, especially the revision, but another pair of eyes will nearly always find mistakes you don't spot.

Another factor to remember is that the buck stops with you. If the work is badly done with serious legal or medical consequences, for example, you may be liable. You may even want to consider taking out insurance.

Unlike a translator who is actually doing the job, it should be remembered that an outsourcer who is managing a project between the translator, proofreader (etc.) and the end client can actually apply a discount for the end client if they wish. This is because their workload will be more or less the same for big or small projects. You should be wary of passing a discount onto the translator by cutting their fees, however, since their workload will of course depend mostly on the size of the project. (We shall come back to this concept later.)

Note that having trustworthy translation partners in your language pairs and specialisations is always useful in order to bid for big jobs, too. You can even present yourself to direct clients and agencies as a team with translators and proofreaders.

Too much work?

Of course, at the end of the day, if you find that you are becoming constantly inundated with work 24/7, there is a simple alternative to outsourcing that follows the laws of supply and demand applicable to all professions: raise your fees!

To avoid overcrowding, a successful restaurant can also either open new ones or put up its prices. The fact that you have so much work coming in probably means you're doing a good job, so you've earned it.

"How much do you charge?"

This is obviously one of the first questions an end client will ask you and one which you should be prepared for since your livelihood depends on it. Firstly, it is wise to ask yourself the question "How much *can I charge*?" The answer to this in the short term depends on your skills as a salesperson and a negotiator (if you consider your fees negotiable), and in the long term on your skills as a translator and partner to your client.

Calculating the fee

Most translation jobs I do are charged per word of source text (i.e. the original text from which you are translating), though from German or other languages it makes more sense to charge per line, characters or some other system. This is largely because it is easier for the client to understand this method of payment per unit of text, though it does have the disadvantage of treating the text like a commodity. Most products and services in the market are charged per quantity, sometimes with discounts for a large amount, and clients often see translation in the same way. Even so, the quality (and level of specialisation) will also affect the price, as with commodities. Look at the following texts and decide for yourself how much you would charge per word for each:

There is a pretty beach 5 minutes' walk from the hotel. A bus stops in front of the hotel every hour to go to the town centre. We have a nursery for babies and small children (ask at reception). Pets not allowed.

Flat-based soup bowl decorated in cobalt blue under the tin-glazed cream white surface, with zones made blue by the diffusion of the oxide (lustreware). It is decorated with bryony and small primroses.

Brachial plexus trauma injury is related to trauma during jugular cannulation, plexus stretching and during the dissection of the internal mammary artery that requires extreme retraction of the chest wall.

The first thing you will have noticed is that the price should vary according to the kind of text you are translating. This is clearly because each text will take you a different amount of time (and level of specialisation) to translate. This is the key to the price you should charge: time. Whereas your client will usually want to hear the fee in terms of price per word, you will have to calculate that fee based on how much you wish or need to earn per hour. And to do that, we need to consider the big picture: how much do you wish to earn a year? We have to take into account how many hours we can and should work a week (and hence per year), how much holiday time we wish to take off, taxes, expenditure, etc. Sit down with an Excel document for a while and work out how much money you need to make a year for your business to be viable by comparing how many hours you are willing or able to work a year and how many words of text on average you are able to translate, revise and proofread per hour. (Take into account holiday periods, tax, etc.) This should finally give you an idea of the average fee per word you should be charging. And remember that this is just your basic fee for a normal text. Specialised texts and rush jobs will cost extra, for example.

The urgent fee

As with translators who never say "no", those who do not apply an urgency fee run the risk of becoming the client's or agency's last resort, the one who will accept the jobs others don't want at no extra charge, even at the weekend or late in the evening in your time zone.

And again, there is also the question of honesty: do you really have time to do a good job? If not, at least warn the client.

<u>The format fee</u>

Another reason for adding a surcharge to your base fee is the format of the source text. Is it a messily photocopied and scanned PDF, for example? Again, you need to consider how much longer it will take to do the translation because of this format (and teach the client the importance of sending you texts in a workable format) and calculate your per-word fee accordingly. Sometimes clients miraculously "discover" that they do actually have the document in Word format when you raise the fee! You may also decide to invest in OCR software (Optical Character Recognition) such as ABBYY or OmniPage to convert PDFs and scanned documents to Word, for example (although this still takes time and is an investment on your part which should be reflected in the fee). Many scanners/printers also come with standard OCR software, so check if you have it already.

All price hikes apply equally to agencies as well as to direct clients. If an agency is charging its end clients too low, it needs to be aware of this and learn to negotiate better fees, just as freelancers do.

<u>Charge per hour?</u>

Some translators even charge per hour for their work, thereby perfectly relating the level of difficulty in doing the translation with the final fee charged. You may be able to do this with clients who know and trust you, though the per-hour fee is usually better applied to proofreading work. Obviously, a badly written or translated text, possibly mangled by an online machine translator, will take far longer to proofread (or even re-do from scratch) than a well-written or translated text. Charging per hour will reflect the amount of work you need to do (and thereby teach the client the importance of sending you well-written texts if they don't want the fee to escalate!).

The client needs to know that proofreading a machine translation or a translation by a non-professional on their staff will usually lead to quality so low that the translator will need more time to compare it to the source text to check the translation is correct. Such poor translation or direct writing may even lead to mistakes later on in the process or that the proofreader may not spot (especially if they have no source text for comparison). You need to warn the client against doing a "home-made" translation of their own text for you to then "clean up a bit" afterwards.

Charging per hour is a possible way of showing your clients this principle; when they realise that it costs more to clean up a poor text (because it takes longer) than to translate it with better results, the common sense conclusion will be to pay you to translate it instead. They will save themselves time, effort and money.

There is also another option open to you if you get a badly written source text to translate or a badly translated target text to proofread, which we shall look at a few pages further on.

Transcreation

There are cases where simply translating the source text will not be enough to have the desired effect on the target readers. Indeed, there may even be cases where the effect may be totally undesired (e.g. advertising with scantily clad young people may be seen as extremely offensive in some cultures). Advise your client.

Advertising is a classic case where long phone calls with the client may be necessary to understand precisely what they're looking for. Indeed, I sometimes find it may be wise to advise my clients to look for a marketing agency in their target country to design an entire campaign from scratch there instead of simply translating a campaign originally designed for their home country.

Entire marketing teams are sometimes hired to come up with a simple slogan of three or four words, costing hundreds of thousands of euros. If we talk about "fee per word" in such cases, this is clearly irrelevant! Again, the time and expertise employed is what counts.

If you check out the websites of successful multinationals such as Coca Cola, you'll find that their pages for China or the UK are not just the same text in different languages; they are entirely different in terms of content, graphic design, etc. This is because they have been completely adapted to the local market, but it is not just *localisation* of the text. This is *transcreation*: creating the entire content from scratch for different target readers or purposes. (The fees charged can and should be the same as those of the client's country; don't give discounts for "cheaper" target countries. If a UK company wants an ad in India, it should pay UK fees.)

<u>Source text quality</u>

As mentioned above, it is wise to point out to clients that simply proofreading a badly translated text (perhaps translated by an unqualified, non-native, non-translator intern or even Google) will probably lead to a lower quality target text. Explain to the client that it is much better for them to create an excellent original text in their native language with all of the rich, detailed vocabulary and grammatical nuances their language allows, which can then translate for the same effect in the target language, than to send you a poorly written text to simply clean up basic mistakes. A way to help the client see this without wasting your time is to first send them corrections and comments only on the first bad paragraph.

I myself now generally refuse to accept very badly written texts for me to translate, proofread, revise or review, simply because I have realised that the quality of the source text is so low (and consequently the quality of the target text, due to the principle of "polishing turds"!) that it is not worth my time or their money. Note that a badly written text may not even be the work of a non-native author; as translators know, many people write terribly in their own language! In addition to charging per hour instead of per word, another option is to suggest that a professional, native colleague of yours rewrite the source text well.

Above all, don't just get silently frustrated at a badly written text. Our clients are not professionals of the written word, which is why they (should) turn to us in the first place. Once again, it is a case of teaching the client to help themselves to produce a good translation, as well as a question of professional ethics: non-native, non-translators should not be writing texts in languages other than their mother tongue; that's *our* job.

When you go to the hairdresser's, you don't take a pair of scissors with you to start it off and let the professional "tidy it up" afterwards. Nor do you take food to a restaurant for the chef to cook, or meddle with your car before handing it over to the mechanic. The client should let the professional do their job to get professional results. Teach them this.

Perhaps it is worth mentioning at this point an observation I have made over my years in freelance translation: clients with very poorly written source texts who aren't bothered about improving them generally don't pay well. This is no coincidence; whether it's for their website, a newsletter to their end clients or a contract for doing business in another country, it's quite possible that a client who doesn't care about the quality of their text (source or target) probably doesn't care about other aspects of their business, either. It has a domino effect that goes both ways: their end clients will presumably not be expecting or looking for great quality, either, and will be expecting to pay an accordingly low price. The fact is that a badly written text is indicative that the author or have-a-go translator isn't too professional, for whatever reason, and as a result they are less likely to be very meticulous in other matters such as their own line of business (including payment practices). This is of course a huge generalisation depending somewhat on the particular professional or social group, intended readers or the country's level of education, but in my experience a dreadful source text can act as a warning that should set your alarm bells ringing about a possible cheapskate, dodgy client. We all know that the most obvious email scams are usually badly written, for example. A sloppy text is often created by a sloppy client.[3]

---

[3] Having said all of this, if on the other hand the source text or the text you have been sent to proofread is well written, then let the client or agency know

<u>Small jobs</u>

It is also wise to have a **minimum fee** for small jobs to make sure clients don't keep sending you little sentences or paragraphs all day. Each job, however small, means you have to stop other jobs to attend to it, invoice it etc. This minimum fee accounts for all the extra time involved, not just the translation itself.

<u>Round numbers</u>

Most clients like to hear the fee estimate in terms of a fee per word/line/character or hour, especially if it's the first time they are buying translation services. However, if the job you're being asked to do involves not only translation or revision but also DTP[4], the use of special software (e.g. for subtitling) or some kind of extra service (e.g. uploading the translation to a website), then bear in mind that it has been shown that customers in any market generally prefer to hear neat, round numbers, not €587.23. So round the quote up or down if they need a set price before the job begins, even if this includes a breakdown of the services provided.

---

this, too. We can also give them good news, which is equally useful to them and much more welcome!

[4] Desktop publishing.

Discounts and special payment arrangements

You may decide to waive the minimum fee or urgency fee once in a while for a good, regular, client, but make sure they know this is the exception to the rule. Remember: the urgency fee not only exists to make more money. It is there to teach the client that good translation takes time. Explain to them what is involved if necessary, so that they understand the reasons why.

Some clients may ask you to give them a discount for a large volume of work, as if they were buying a commodity in bulk. This may make sense when selling goods, but not so much when selling services, since a lot of translation work also means committing yourself to one client for a long time. Other, better paid jobs may appear which you will then have to reject in order to continue working on the long project, and you need to be compensated for this possibility. In other words, it is not advisable to drop your fees for a large volume of work unless you really do need it.

Another reason some agencies ask for a discount may be based on the amount of fuzzy matches[5] in the text. It is entirely up to you if you accept this. We should remember that 100% matches are not necessarily correct in the specific context where they appear and so they will still need to be proofread anyhow. Also, changes made in the final proofreading of past translated texts will often not then appear in the translation memory (and thus in the fuzzy matches) unless the original translator makes a point of inserting them. Such discounts will not take this into account, either.

_____

[5] Partial matches with previously translated sections of text indicated by translation software.

Another factor you may wish to consider is asking for 50% up front for completely new clients with long projects, or at least having the project paid in timely instalments. We shouldn't exaggerate the amount of bad payers out there (they are a small minority), but it's best to cover your back and not to let your client's debt accumulate. I know a translator who checked out an agency on the ProZ Blue Board (a well-known list where translators can comment on their experience of agencies and outsourcers) and found it to have a lot of bad remarks. He told them that given this situation, he would only do the job if they paid him 100% up front. They did.

Yet another example of how simple communication and honesty can lead to a good working relationship.

Raising your fees

As in all professions, from time to time we also have to raise our fees in line with general inflation at least. Few agencies and even fewer end clients will raise your fees voluntarily, so it is up to you to do this yourself. But how do you go about it?

Well, firstly you should avoid giving your client nasty surprises. Try to raise your fees at the same time of year, either at the beginning of the calendar year or just after the country's holiday period, for example. It may also be worthwhile warning them a couple of months in advance.

If it's a good client you like working for, maybe you could just suggest a raise by saying something like, "How much are you paying this year?" This way, the ball is in their court and they should eventually realise they are going to lose you if they don't raise your fees after a few years. The important point here is that by simply asking the question you are letting your client know that you are thinking about your fees and not just blindly accepting what they are offering you. If you don't ask, you won't get.

If the client is a low payer whose work you don't particularly like anyhow, you can simply state your new fees. If they refuse, at least you haven't lost a client that really matters to you in any case.

At the end of the day, though, if you truly want to raise your fees above inflation in the long term, in addition to looking for better, direct clients, the surest way to be able to do so is to improve your translation and other skills we shall look at in this book. There is no substitute for quality.

Confirming the fee

Another piece of advice is to put your agreed payment deadline on the invoice if you like, so again the client has it in writing. You should also prepare a neat PDF with all of your payment, tax and bank details (along with a memorable logo or brand), so you don't have to keep writing it out every time a client asks you for such information.

If you have decided on the fee for a project over the phone, send the client a confirmation email anyway so they also have it in writing to avoid future disagreements.[6]

You may wish to ask new clients for a purchase order, too, if they haven't sent you one. This should show the service being requested by the client, preferably with a word count so that if they make significant changes to the text later you can point out that these represent another job.

---

[6] Note, however, that some cultures prefer spoken agreements and may think you don't trust them if you do this (e.g. parts of Asia, the Middle East and Africa). You'll have to gauge this as you negotiate on the phone.

<u>Specialisation</u>

Specialising in a subject is a clear way to raise your fees in the long term. Too many translators get stuck on a treadmill of low fees offered by clients and agencies simply because many other translators provide the same service, so there is great competition. We need to turn this attitude on its head and think what *we can offer our clients* that other translators can't. Whether this means learning to streamline or sharpen our work with software (e.g. Dragon, Xbench, Verifika, etc.) or techniques (e.g. touch typing, hotkeys), studying a specialisation (there is a millionaire freelance translator who translates very specific texts about superconductors for lucrative corporate clients) or providing an extra service (e.g. DTP), if you can provide a more specialised service, you can demand higher fees.

In order to do so, you can go on courses to study all of these possibilities. Remember: *spending* time and money is not the same as *investing* them.

<u>Spreading risk</u>

Although it is advisable to specialise if we wish to be able to raise our fees, we should also avoid putting all our eggs into one basket. We should always be on the lookout for new clients who may provide better pay and conditions. Indeed, the best time to look for new clients is when we are doing fine, not five minutes after our sole income-provider finds a cheaper translator or goes bust. It is when things are going well that we can go about the job hunt patiently and professionally, while honing our specialist skills.

It is far better to be indispensable to clients who are dispensable to us than to be dispensable to clients who are indispensable to us.

Considerations beyond the fee

Finally, we may also ask ourselves if it is only the fee that matters when accepting or rejecting work. One of my clients is an NGO working for a good cause, so I have a special, lower fee for them. The work is also fairly easy and interesting, and the people I work with are very pleasant and understanding.

On the other hand, you may get work that you simply don't enjoy. Maybe it's an extremely boring list of mechanical parts with little context, for example. In this case, you may decide to apply a "pain-in-the-neck" surcharge (but don't tell your client you call it this!) to make it worth your while.

"Are you qualified?"

What to put on a CV

When you walk into a mechanic's garage or a dentist's surgery and they begin to talk to you in their professional jargon, it is sometimes reassuring to see the wall plastered with framed certificates. You have no idea what these certificates are, but presumably the service-provider has had some professional training to earn them.

Similarly, new direct clients often like to have this reassurance and so ask this question. The problem for older translators is that translation and interpreting degrees are actually a rather recent phenomenon. Many of the more experienced translators in business today actually began through other channels. There are engineers and nurses, for example, who on having lived and worked in different countries for many years have acquired invaluable, specialised vocabulary and above all a feel for the culture of their professions in different countries. Indeed, these days it can be quite difficult to make a living in translation if you do not have some kind of specialisation (specific fields of law, medicine, finance etc.).

Therefore, it is a good idea to put any qualification that may be relevant to specific fields of translation on your CV. There are also courses for specific translation fields you can attend. Check out translation associations' websites and look for specialised courses, seminars and congresses.

Most professional translation associations will also ask you for your credentials as a translator or at least proof of having worked officially as such for a certain period of time. By joining them, this will also thus act as an endorsement of your ability as a translator.

Again, this should go on your CV and you may have permission to use their logo as a member (ask first and only use it as an individual member, not confusing it with your company if you have one, unless it is an association of companies). This shows at the very least that you take your job seriously enough to become a member of an association (and pay for it) and indicates that you are still in business.

Recent courses and congresses should also go on your CV if only to show, again, that you are still in business. If you got your translation degree ten years ago, potential clients may wonder what you have been doing since then. Even if you have been doing something supposedly unrelated to pure translation, such as working in an export department of a multinational, this will probably still also be relevant to a specialisation and shows you can hold down a job, so put it in there. (Some job descriptions say nothing about translation when it is actually what they involve. I have friends with degrees in translation who bemoan the fact they are not freelance translators today, yet when I ask them what they do in their current jobs in all sorts of companies, they reply "Oh, I translate their emails, reports and so on…" In other words, they are indeed translators! Such work can easily go on their CV described as a translation job.)

Courses on translation software and the kind of software you use should also go on CVs you send to agencies. Again, these indicate that you take your profession seriously and are prepared to pay for the tools of the trade and ongoing training. Direct clients may even be swayed by simply seeing that you are a paying member of a website such as ProZ.com (giving you access to extra, useful services that are not available to non-paying members), indicated simply by a blue ribbon next to your name. (There is even the ProZ Certified scheme indicated by a rosette next to your name. Though such "qualifications" may be of limited merit, rather than ask "Why bother?", ask yourself "Why not?". Potential direct clients from outside the profession will inevitably choose a "ProZ certified" translator on the website over one who isn't.)

Finally, you may wish to put a professional photo of yourself on your CV, which we will study in more detail later, in order to add a human, friendly touch.

<u>Your CV file</u>

Another useful tip is to put what you do on your CV's actual file name (e.g. ES>EN Court_Interpreter.doc or FR>EN Medical_translator.pdf). This way, when an agency or outsourcer needs your services, they can easily find your CV instead of having to wade through your document to discover if you are suitable. I would also recommend having a CV of not more than one page; most outsourcers simply do not have the time to look through more, especially if they have an urgent job to allocate.

<u>Beyond the CV</u>

It may even be advisable to not create a CV at all, but rather a well-designed, eye-catching advertisement, profile (e.g. about.me) or website landing page. We are, after all, individuals that need to act as micro-companies. Once you have caught a potential client or agency's attention, they can ask you for further information, experience and credentials.

When we go to a professional such as a dentist or lawyer, we don't usually ask to see their CV. There are other signs that inspire our trust in their professionalism, experience and renown.

<u>Test translations</u>

Some agencies or outsourcers may ask you for a test translation. This is a rather controversial practice, above all because of the suspicion that unscrupulous people are trying to get a free translation (albeit with scant regard for quality). Such tests should not be of more than a few hundred words. I myself pay for such tests or give a small section of a real translation job if I'm looking for a translator, but I must also say that I have done such tests myself for free and have found some of my best clients this way. As an outsourcer myself, I am aware of the usefulness of such tests. However many qualifications and however much experience is on a translator's CV, the proof is in the pudding, so to speak. By giving a test translation with a reasonable deadline, one can get an idea of how well a translator can do a professional job in a real working situation. It's similar to a restaurant or supermarket giving free samples to see if the customers will like the product and buy more. On the positive side, it can also be a great way of showing potential clients or agencies your skills and knowledge if you lack official qualifications.

A proper test translation should attempt to truly test various aspects of the translator's skills. It may have a time limit, for example, and a few deliberate mistakes of varying kinds (grammatical, factual, etc.) in the source text to see if the translator points them out. It should also be relevant to the specialisation if there is one, and it may even include the odd "untranslatable" term to see what the translator does with it. Do they make any comments or simply send the translation as is?

It's only natural to want to try to ensure a translator with whom you have never worked is going to do a good job. And even then I myself have had my fingers burnt. (I particularly remember one translator to whom I had given a couple of small, paid jobs which she had done satisfactorily, before entrusting her with a book translation—which was a disaster that I had to do again.)

At the end of the day, if you are making a living out of translation then your clients are actually testing you every working day with every job they give you, anyhow. The price you pay for failing these daily "tests" is that you will lose the clients and not be able to make a living out of translation.

Having said all of this, there are still translators with perfectly respectable reservations about doing test translations; you may simply decide you never want to do free sample translations and this is a perfectly acceptable personal decision. Each case should be judged individually anyhow; always try to check out the potential client to see if they are respectable before doing anything for free for them.

Getting experience

If you are just starting out in translation, you may even be tempted to give your services for free to an organisation with a big name that you could then put on your CV. If so, try to do so for something like the Wikipedia, a charity or an NGO that you can then point to as an example of your work, rather than for such corporate giants as Facebook. Such companies have more than enough money to pay a huge team of professional translators a decent salary and should be encouraged to do so, instead of relying on crowd translation which, as we shall see later, is also a controversial area.

Obviously, a degree in translation would be the best option when a client asks you about the title of this page. I consider a university degree in translation to be like spending a few years training in an excellent agency. Talking of which, in-house training in an agency is also another way of gaining bona-fide, invaluable experience of the translation process.

And of course, working for respectable agencies as a freelance translator will be useful experience to show to potential direct clients as you build up your portfolio of them.[7]

---

[7] Another option to get experience is to find a mentor. See the "Starting Out" section.

Recommendations

And talking of experience, nothing speaks more highly of a service provider than satisfied customers, like those restaurants packed with locals, or the local friend who recommends the mechanic they've been using for years. So, put your past clients on your CV, LinkedIn profile, ProZ WWAs, etc. to show potential clients that others have been satisfied with your work, asking them to recommend you publicly.

The flip side to recommendations, however, is seen in the dreaded blacklists that can bring down reputations. This is something we obviously want to avoid at all costs and is an area that needs to be treated with the utmost care.

<u>A word about blacklists</u>

Take a look at these two blacklist entries from disgruntled translators, complaining about the same agency for the same reasons:

"They lied about the payment deadlines. Bad communicators. Their staff don't know how to bill. Very unprofessional."

"Payment was made a month after the agreed deadline. Three days to answer my questions about the text. Some mistakes in the bill had to be rectified."

What is the big difference between these two comments? Well, if we're going to be honest, the first quote is simply an insult. The second, however, limits itself to the facts. This is obviously wiser. It allows the agency to justify the problems if it can. Who knows, maybe the project manager had an accident or was giving birth (!), their end client was unresponsive, they got a computer virus, their bank made a mistake…You may even have to be honest and recognise that you didn't do the best job in your life. The point is, the agency may have reasonable, justified reasons for the problems, and by limiting yourself to the facts they can explain this. More importantly, other translators can see exactly why you are complaining, instead of giving the impression that you are just whinging.

Obviously, we must remember that other translators and agencies will see your blacklist entry. If it is simply an insult, they may well think twice about working with you. In life in general, insults backfire. They are life's "own goals", often doing more damage to those who proffer them than to those on the receiving end. Remember also that agencies and clients can change over the years. They may hire a new project manager, improve their working methods and so on. Nevertheless, your comment will stay on the net *forever*. Other translators and agencies reading your comments in future years may be puzzled as to why you complained if you don't give the reasons.

It is also wise to remember that, in the end, our working relationships are never truly virtual. There is always (or should be) a human on the other side of your computer screen, with their own personal problems and stresses. You may even bump into them one day at a congress, or someone who knows them.

Finally, my advice to outsourcers who have had a bad experience with a translator is this: pay up, thank them, say goodbye and never call them again. Obviously, there will be trouble if the amount of payment involved is rather large, but for this reason a paid test translation or at least a smaller initial job should be done first to check out the translator's worthiness. The danger of appearing on a blacklist for non-payment may cost you far more money in lost work in future.

For some strange reason, blacklists only ever seem to mention money as opposed to many other reasons for a soured working relationship. Perhaps we should also mention other aspects of professionalism.[8] Furthermore, we should not forget that as well as naming to shame we can also name for fame. In other words, we can also highlight good agencies and clients as well as the problematic ones, helping create a good vibe with them that will also reflect well on yourself when others see your positive attitude.

---

[8] The Proz.com Blue Board has improved in this respect, allowing users to mention other aspects.

To sum up, then, *never make enemies*. Never insult. Just give the facts. Remember that agencies and clients may have justified reasons. In addition, don't answer in the heat of the moment. Just as you shouldn't go on Facebook late at night after a few glasses of wine, an overheated reaction on a blacklist after a rush of blood to the head may have long-lasting consequences. Give it a few days and see if you can take out some of those ill-sounding adjectives at least.

And above all, remember that whatever you put on the internet stays there *forever*.

Beyond the Ads: Visibility

How often do you click on Google Ads? Exactly. That's why I'm not going to advise you to use them.

Have you ever seen a thirty-second commercial for a car on TV and thought to yourself "I must go out and buy that car tomorrow"? Probably not. Why then, do the giants of the automotive industry spend hundreds of millions of euros on TV campaigns every year? Why do they put posters at bus stops, ads on hoardings and billboards and even ads on the radio, if they know that people do not buy their cars after merely seeing or hearing a small ad? The answer to this, in a word, is: *constancy*. We can all probably name about seven or eight famous car manufacturers, yet there are actually hundreds. So, when we do finally take the decision to buy a new car, there are several that we immediately consider as big, reliable household names because we see their advertising everywhere. Fortunately, even freelancers can play this game rather more cheaply on a smaller scale by aiming our services at niche markets—and more so in the age of the internet.

It is no great secret that one way of getting yourself known in the translation world is by taking part in forums on the social networks (Facebook, LinkedIn, Twitter, ProZ, etc.), particularly if you're capable of giving good advice or even simply posting some interesting links related to translation and interpreting. But remember that the trick lies in constancy. You may not have time to spend hours every day trying to build up your image on the social networks, but try to spend a few minutes a day at least to take part in a translation-related topic or even merely to congratulate a colleague for something they have said or done. The important thing is to keep your visibility constant so that others in the profession know and remember who you are when they have a job that is suitable for you.

It's also important that others should be aware of your language combinations and specialisations, so try to drop these into your comments etc. once in a while. You may take a photo of yourself by a famous monument in your city or on your travels to a country that speaks one of your languages so that people remember your language pairs or your city of residence when there's an interpreting job there. I sometimes mention funny situations with my lawyer clients and post photos of the beach where I live in Spain, which in addition to making my colleagues jealous also reminds them that I live in Spain and that Spanish is one of my languages!

Get involved in forums and topics relevant to your profile and specialisations, too, even if they are niches. They can also be useful for asking questions when you have a query about specialised terminology. Though having thousands of followers may be good for your ego, on a professional level it's no use if they don't know what you do for a living and will never give you work or recommend you. Make sure your professional networks are useful.

Getting involved in forums and circles that are not related directly to translation or interpreting, but which are related solely to your specialisations, can be very useful for finding direct clients. For example, if you specialise in translations for the tourist industry, you may get involved in sites related to the hotel and catering industry. Again, make sure they know you are a translator. This way, you may be the only translator they know or remember when they need a translation or simply linguistic advice. It is far easier to stand out from the crowd when you are the only translator in the forum!

You may also do this locally in person, for example at international trade fairs related to a specialisation of yours. Let's say there's a furniture exhibition in town and you happen to be something of an expert in translations about interior design. Why not pop by with your business cards and chat to some of the representatives at the stands? Obviously, you should avoid the hard sell. Take an interest in their stand and their products, perhaps even as a potential buyer, before leaving them your card and explaining what you do. It is far easier to remember someone you've met in person.

Business cards

For in-person situations, have your business cards9 on you at all times. Keep them in your wallet or handbag along with your keys, your money and your phone.

One advantage of our profession is that absolutely anybody may need our services at some time. Our clients can come from all walks of life; you never know who is going to be a customer of yours one day. Whenever you are at a party or meet someone new, make sure you don't say goodbye without them knowing that you're a translator. In fact, do the profession a favour and explain what it is we do! For the few cents that a piece of card costs, you may get a client worth thousands a year.

It is useful to have two kinds of business cards aimed at two different kinds of potential clients: one for direct clients unrelated to the translation profession and one for translation and interpreting colleagues and agencies. The card for direct clients

---

[9] You can get cheap, professional cards at www.Vistaprint.com or www.moo.com.

should make it clear you are a linguist (e.g. flags representing your languages), whereas the card for colleagues needs to set you apart in some other way (e.g. a picture of a stethoscope if you specialise in medical translation).

We should carry our direct client cards on us at all times for chance encounters and especially at specialised events such as trade fairs for tourism, cuisine, etc. The cards for colleagues and agencies are more for translation congresses and gatherings.

It may also be an idea to put a photo of yourself on your card. After a two-minute chat, it will be difficult years later for your potential client to recall who you are if there is no photo. Needless to say, it should be a professional one; not a photo of you on holiday.[10]

You may also consider leaving some space on the card to write something by hand before giving it to someone, thereby giving them some useful information you've just been talking about or simply adding a personal touch. This can be another reason for them to keep your card and remember who you are.

---

[10] Some countries and business cultures don't like photos on cards or CVs; try to find out what's best in your countries' and specialisations' cultures. Note that actually *soliciting* a photo from potential business partners is not a good idea as it may arouse suspicions of prejudice based on physical traits, etc. Also remember that personal photos and image are more applicable to freelancers, not so much to companies, which are more interested in promoting their brand and logo rather than individual employees who may leave next year. If you are aiming to create and grow a company, maybe you should be looking more at plugging your logo and brand etc.

Obviously, your language pairs are the most essential information that must go on your card, as well as any specialisation. Interpreters without much mobility may also wish to state their geographical area of residence, too.

<u>The elevator speech</u>

Similar considerations as for business cards can be made when meeting potential clients or colleagues for the first time. First impressions count, so why not prepare yours beforehand?

The elevator speech or pitch is one you can supposedly rattle off in the minute you are in an elevator with a potential client, for example. If we're talking to a non-translator, then we can allay their fears and pre-empt society's general ignorance of our profession by answering the usual questions we hear, including information such as this in a coherent narrative you can invent for yourself:

- Translators write; interpreters speak.

- Just because someone speaks languages well, doesn't make them a translator.

- Machine translation will put human translators out of business who translate like machines. (Can a machine write Macbeth? Humans read and write the text, so only a human translator can tell if the message is right.)

- Translators also have excellent writing and editing skills, as well as being great at localisation.

- Translators don't necessarily know lots of languages, but they specialise (e.g. financial or medical translators). "For example, my specialisation is..."

Obviously, most of these points are already known by our colleagues, so when we meet them we need a different set of points, letting them know useful information while setting yourself apart in some way. For example:

- Your language pairs (source and target).

- Relevant qualifications and experience.

- Your specialisations.

- Where you are based.

- Places you've lived.

- Something 'different' about you (e.g. hobby unrelated to translation).

Gimmicks

It is quite cheap to produce pens, pencils, etc. from local business suppliers with your contact information or website URL on them. You may even put a mysterious link on them to a well-prepared landing page all about you (e.g. about.me, Google+, LinkedIn, ProZ profile). Use a different URL such as those generated via *bit.ly* or *Hootsuite* to pique the recipient's interest.

Commercial branding

If you prefer to use a brand name other than your real name, make sure it is related to the profession or your specialisation. It should give an instant idea of the service you provide. However catchy your brand or business name sounds, if it's unrelated to your services it will not attract the right people. It may well attract many followers on Twitter and "likes" on Facebook, but if they're not potential clients or colleagues this will serve little purpose other than to boost your ego.

It should also be relatively easy to pronounce and remember in your potential clients' working languages.

And don't spend too long thinking up the name anyhow. Twitter, Facebook, Google and ProZ are not exactly fantastic, eye-catching names, nor do they even indicate the service they provide. They don't need to. If you provide a good service and use the social networks well, the right people will find you.

I myself have a name that is not exactly exotic (!), but have had no problem in making myself known in the world of professional translation.

Your name or brand alone will not make you famous in your niche, but you can make it famous.

Sharing knowledge

It goes without saying that if you have some useful insights to share with your colleagues, whether they are about software, proofreading techniques or terminology searches, you can also write a blog or post on relevant ones, or even send an entire article for publication in renowned translation blogs or journals.

There are those who prefer to hoard their 'secret formulae', but by helping your colleagues you are also advertising to them that you are a capable professional with good working practices. They'll remember you.

<u>Proofread, proofread and proofread</u>

Clearly, you need to take great care with your proofreading before publishing or simply posting *anything* on the net, whether it's an article you've written or a quick reply in Facebook.

I have been horrified to see simple mistakes by translators in some forums. Some have given the excuse that they were writing in a hurry to post a job on their smartphone with a different language keypad, for example, but I'm afraid this is still no excuse for writing badly in your native language in our profession. Your phone or keyboard needs to be set up (or you need to know how to adapt it) to write flawlessly. A brief tip for urgent proofreading is to change the format or font in which you've written the text, for example, to italics. On seeing the text differently, glaring errors stand out more; it's as if you're reading a different text. Tests have proven this to work: ow.ly/YEj9K. (For more serious proofreading, printing out the text on paper sometimes helps for similar reasons.) Failing all of this, at the very least explain the reason for the bad quality of the text at the very beginning.

The same clearly goes for answering job offers. Be prepared to write well at all times, even when texting people. Writing well is your profession and every time you do so is an example of your work. Some non-translators I know joke about the fact that I write so well with correct punctuation even in small phone texts—but they never forget that's what I do for a living. I'd rather people make fun of me for writing well than for writing badly—and remember me for it.

Your words are always a sample of the product you sell. It should go without saying that you must proofread everything you write in your working target language to ensure the grammar and punctuation is impeccable. Thousands of your colleagues and potential customers are watching. Speed is no excuse.

Everything is advertising

As communication professionals, all contact we have with clients and colleagues is inevitably advertising for our services. Your voice on the phone, your instant messages, your emails, your invoices, etc. should all be well polished. Prepare a well-written footer for your emails with relevant contact information, qualifications and association memberships (if you have permission). Put your bank and billing details on a well-designed PDF with a logo if you have one.

We are professional communicators. All of our communication advertises ourselves. Make it flawless.

Professional associations

As mentioned before, belonging to a professional translators' association can act as an endorsement of sorts in the face of potential clients. It shows at the very least that you take your job seriously enough to become a member of an association (and pay for it). There are sometimes local associations and nearly always national and international ones that may interest you, so you can go global and local with the respective advantages that such concepts imply. Being in touch with other professionals also helps if you have a query about software, jobs or any problem related to the profession. They can provide you with a profile on their websites for potential clients to find you, too.

Good associations also help dignify the profession in general by promoting good practices, defending professionals' interests, promoting the profession in the eyes of the general public (and potential clients) and providing ongoing training. So it's worth supporting them!

Local associations and events

The benefit of local associations is that you have more opportunities to get to know your local colleagues in person at workshops, general meetings or even social gatherings at certain times of year, all organised by the association. It is far easier to trust people you have met in person. They are no longer just a name on a computer screen and can become more like friends. (You may even like to know you can go and see bad payers in person if necessary!) Some clients also feel safer knowing that you are nearby and may even like to chat about a large project in person over a coffee or at their office. In short, there is simple human trust gained by meeting your colleagues or clients in person, or at least knowing that they are nearby. It is also far easier to take in-person courses when they are local. If there is no local association in your area, you may even consider organising an informal gathering yourself via another professional business association or a ProZ "powwow" (www.ProZ.com/powwows) to meet your local colleagues and swap business cards. Another possibility is to set one up via a translators' forum through LinkedIn, Twitter or Facebook. Remember to put all of your professional profile pages on your business cards and email footers. It's far easier for clients to click on these links than to read your CV in depth.

A translator friend of mine at an international congress once complained to me, "There are never any translators' activities in my area," to which I replied, "Well then, you need to set one up yourself."

She did so the following month, and about thirty local translators turned up! Even so, if few colleagues turn up, you do not need to consider this a failure. (One of my pet mantras is: "*The only true failure is to do nothing*.") Take photos, write a blog entry about it and make sure it has a much bigger impact in the virtual social networks than it did in person anyhow. (After seeing that, the next time others will come after realising what they've missed!)

International associations

One big advantage of international associations is obviously the fact that you can get in touch with colleagues and agencies in the countries of your language pairs as well as others who may be able to help you out with other languages on bigger projects or if you wish to start outsourcing seriously. Their congresses and seminars usually have a far wider impact on the social networks, too, so try to get involved both *in situ* and in relevant forums, or even write up a post about it afterwards.

You should also try to attend some events in your source language countries anyway, since you will be in a minority in your language combination as a native target language speaker. You will thus stand out a little and find many potential colleagues to share work with you in your language pair's direction.

SEO (Search Engine Optimisation)

Here is my advice about search engine optimisation: unless you're aiming for a niche market, don't bother too much since it's already been done for you. By this I mean that however much you try to plug your website or blog via your own channels, it will never be nearly as big as Twitter, Google+, Facebook or even ProZ (the latter is among the top twenty websites in the world, not just for translation). It is far wiser, simpler and cheaper to stand on the shoulders of giants than to become a giant yourself. By all means use the usual tricks, Google's Search Console etc. to boost your SEO, particularly for your specialisations, but do not attempt to re-invent the wheel unless you really believe you are the next Mark Zuckerberg.

Here's an example of what I mean. Let's say you're doing a translation on the manufacture of Persian rugs and you come across an excellent glossary from an obscure Iranian rug manufacturer's website. If you then post a link to this glossary with a short explanation (and your own email address, etc.) in a big forum or even ProZ, the next time somebody looks up such information or a translation for an expression related to Persian rugs, the first entry to appear on their search via Google, for example, will not be the small Iranian company's website but the entry you have posted on a much bigger website, an internet giant. There are also ways to upload a lot of information and text to such websites (search engines are not so interested in text quality but quantity).

If you are serious about doing your own SEO, however, here are a few tips. Don't forget to use a lot of keywords in your social network profiles and change them regularly. Avoid using functions such as text that moves across the page in your keywords, as search engines have more difficulty in using them. Bold text works better in searches. Give your uploaded image documents names and links. Use NameChk.com to see if your desired username is already taken in the social networks. Use Audiense.com, Twitdom and Klout to check out your potential and current audience. And avoid generic links such as "click here"; use "click name".

Your own .com?

It's always good to have your own website to show off your business to the world, but for freelancers it is usually more of an extension to your CV or a great ad as opposed to a way of attracting new clients. Potential clients will nearly always find you via the internet giants, then look at your website to see who you are and how professional you are. At the very least, you should have a domain name to be taken seriously, not an email address such as Red_Devil69@yahoo.mn. Your personal domain name can be as cheap as €10 a year. Check out www.DomainsInSeconds.com, www.joker.com or www.GoDaddy.com. For hosting, you could try www1and1.com, and for fast website building, there is www.Weebly.com, www.NetworkSolutions.com and of course WordPress.

The social networks

Social networks have always existed since long before the internet appeared. With the advent of modern communications, many seem to have forgotten the basics of human interaction, or believe that they have changed. In fact, pretty much the same eternal rules apply when making and keeping good social networks: a decent appearance, friendliness, honesty, etc. I repeat: there is always a human (or maybe thousands) on the other side of the screen, so treat them as you like to be treated yourself with common decency, politeness and respect.

Take our appearance: how would you feel if you went to a job interview and those asking you the questions hid behind a screen, not showing you their face? It'd seem a bit creepy, right? You'd probably mistrust such people. The same applies to those who never show their face or a photo of themselves on the net.

Equally, if you conducted a job interview and your potential work colleagues arrived wearing very casual clothes or enjoying a glass of wine, you might be a little taken aback (depending on the kind of profession, of course; in tourism or oenology it may be acceptable). Clearly, we would expect our interlocutor's appearance to be professional and at least pleasant. The same goes for our online image and photos. At the very least, get a passport-style photo wearing formal clothes and a big smile. Or better still, pay a professional photographer or studio to take those photos that are going to be your online image for the next few years.

You would also be surprised if you were interviewing someone for a job and they turned up with their husband, wife or kids to accompany them in the interview. The job concerns you, not your friends, family or pet cat, so keep them out of your professional photos.

In real life, it has been proven that the first impression we make has a very lasting effect on others. Exactly the same is true for the impression you make in human interactions in the digital age. Take good care of it, in person and online.

LinkedIn

A few years ago, LinkedIn was a very static site. It was a little like a business card; you didn't use it very often but if someone asked to see your profile they were not impressed if you didn't have one. Nowadays, however, it is far more dynamic, allowing you to post updates and useful links. The best thing to be said about LinkedIn is that it is an *active* way of finding clients (as opposed to the passive way of hoping clients will find you). You can actively look for professionals involved in your specialisations, chambers of commerce and so on. You could even correct their badly written texts and leave them your contact information! (You should avoid publicly criticising companies anyway, since potential clients may see your criticisms and become wary of hiring you. Be tactful.) It's also possible to ask your LinkedIn contacts to introduce you to interesting new contacts virtually. There are options to request recommendations from your clients and colleagues, too.

Google+

Google+ is also forever gaining ground though still hasn't attained the same reach as Facebook. However, it has the undoubted advantage that Google will clearly favour it in its own search engine rankings, in addition to the plethora of Google-owned and related sites and tools at your disposal that you can keep well connected (e.g. Google Drive, Google Keep, Google Alerts, Boomerang, etc.). Google Input Tools' Chrome Extension can be useful for translators.

Facebook

We cannot forget Facebook, of course. Make yourself a professional profile if you wish, using an address entirely unrelated to your personal mail if you have one (or get one in a few minutes via Gmail or Yahoo). In any case, "friends of friends" can see what you post even if you only have the post open to "friends", so you will need to take care that none of your social friends or family know any of your colleagues, which may be a tall order. My advice is to simply not post anything on Facebook—or anywhere on the internet—that you may not want others to see.

Another idea is simply to run a professional Facebook group with your brand image.

There is also Twitter for those who prefer short, open conversations or to simply post and receive interesting links about the translation world and languages in general. Here are some useful translation-related hashtags in English:

#xl8	Translate (x = trans; l; 8=ate. Variants: #xl8r, #t9r)
#t9n	Translation (T + nine letters (-ranslatio-) + n)
#i18n	Internationalisation
#g11n	Globalisation
#L10n	Localisation
#t9y	Terminology
#1nt	Interpreting

You can also use hashtags related to your specialisations to get known among your potential clients. (If the professionals following such hashtags don't understand the ones listed above, you can explain them to raise awareness about the profession!) They are also useful at congresses to retweet significant messages, whether you are there in person wishing to show the world what's happening or you wish to take a peek at snippets from a congress you can't attend in person.

Statistically, tweets with one or two hashtags get twice as much engagement as tweets with none, whereas tweets with more than two see a drop in interest.

To help manage your Twitter account and to find and target relevant tweets, group those you follow into lists (e.g. freelance translators, agencies, general language, current affairs, your specialisations, etc.) and remember to place them in these lists every time you begin to follow a new one.

One to rule them all...

Again, I stress that the importance in all of these networks is constancy, even if it's only a few minutes a day. Two or three of the giants I've mentioned above may be enough to keep you occupied. You can also use tools such as Hootsuite and Buffer to send scheduled announcements via several platforms at the same time, instead of having to write posts for each social network. This way, you can also post at night when your target or source language readers are awake on the other side of the world (and amaze them at your 24/7 omnipotence!).

If you prefer to keep your social networks completely separate from your work networks, it may be useful to use a different browser for your friends and family, and another for your work contacts (Firefox, Chrome...and maybe Explorer for less-used accounts!) so that you don't have to constantly log in and out of each.

Skype

Skype can be a convenient, unobtrusive way for clients and agencies to get in touch with you at any time via different social networks. In order for it to be truly unobtrusive, you might want to have the option "away" switched on. If you use the option "Do Not Disturb", you might as well log out of Skype altogether, as they won't contact you and you won't be aware if they do anyhow. By stating that you are "away", they can send you a message but they won't expect you to reply immediately, so you can finish the paragraph you're translating (or the coffee you're drinking!).

Note that Hangouts is also similarly useful and Blab can be a good means not only of communicating in groups, but also of giving presentations, etc.

<u>The phone</u>

You can also use Skype, Twitter and Facebook easily on a smartphone, as well as Whatsapp, Viber, Telegram etc. (Telegram is actually better than Whatsapp for sending files etc., but unfortunately most people still use Whatsapp so we need to have it, too.) You can also put a short description and your email or website address in your profiles.

I would certainly advise getting a smartphone if you don't already have one in order to receive job offers anytime, anywhere so as not be tied to the office. There are those who say "I prefer to leave my work behind at the office when I'm not working." However, "leaving your work at the office" is in truth a state of mind. I have translator friends who leave their phone at home or the office, then spend all day worrying about possible missed calls and job offers. Clearly, they have not really left their job at the office at all.

I once took a call from a client who is now one of my best customers while I was out jogging. Let me stress the big difference between accepting work-related messages and actually doing work. If I am dining out with friends at the weekend and I get a message offering me an interesting job, I have no problem in taking 30 seconds to reply, saying: "I can't look at it now but I will do so on Monday morning," for example. In fact, after answering that job offer whilst jogging, I actually continued running on my usual morning route and kept to my routine, had a shower and so on, before actually switching on my computer looking at the work in hand. And most importantly, I never get stressed out about such calls or emails.

Of course, there may be times when it is humanly impossible to do the job or even reply. As I have said before, we should not be afraid to say "no", simply stating our reasons if possible.

Despite all of this advice, there are still clients, agencies and fellow translators who prefer to make a phone call rather than send an email or instant message, for example.

This is fine provided they use the phone efficiently. You don't want them to be calling and interrupting you every twenty minutes with small questions about the text that they could put all together in one email, for example. Nor are you there to chat about life in general during working hours, however friendly your relationship with them. (This also applies to friends and family, who should be aware that although you work from home this does not mean you're available to chat at any time as if it were the weekend; make sure they're aware of your working hours.)

If you have a client who is rather too chatty and calls you constantly, it may be a good idea to apply a policy of only answering the phone at certain times of day (e.g. 12 noon till 1 p.m. and 4.30 p.m. till 5 p.m.). This way, they will end up noting down what they want to say to you and be more effective when they call you. You can even leave an automated message with your email address indicating this policy, saying something like, "Due to an exceptionally busy period / unforeseen circumstances, I will only be available to answer the phone from...".

You should also make it clear as soon as they call you that you are not available for idle chat. Say something like, "I'm quite busy; I've only got a couple of minutes, I'm afraid," immediately after greeting them. If it's truly urgent, two minutes will be enough for them to communicate the basic problem to you. If it isn't, you can direct them to your email.

Some service providers say we should pick up the phone before it rings three times. This may be applicable to big service providers (and translation agencies) with their own phone operators or even call exchanges, but it only seems fair if they are prepared to do the same when we call them. If your client respects you and wants you to do the job, they will contact you in a way that's suitable for you. People who expect you to be available 24/7 and to pick up the phone immediately at any time may not be the kind of people you wish to work with.

There are also particular clients and fields where a certain amount of phone work may be necessary. If the text has little context, you or your client may find that a phone conversation will actually be faster than emails back and forth. Advertising texts in particular may require the client to chat with you for some time to be absolutely clear about the target audience, the underlying message and various nuances of the text, slogans, etc. In this case it may well be wise to set out a fee per hour of phone/Skype time with them, as this is also your working time and all part of the job.

If you find that with your particular specialisation or clients you are getting a little overwhelmed in keeping up with phone calls, check out YourMail or Switch.Co, visual voicemail apps that act like an electronic secretary to filter and handle your calls.

Before, After and During the Translation: Extra Services

<u>"Can you translate a text for us?"</u>

Online translators sometimes face classic problems due to our monolingual, monocultural clients' lack of knowledge about what's involved in the translation process.

The first one can appear when they first contact us, asking simple questions such as "How much will it cost?" or "How long will it take?" without telling us if the text in question is *The Complete Works of Shakespeare* or a small restaurant menu. It's a little like asking a mechanic the same questions without letting them look at your car, or not letting a dentist look at your mouth. Obviously, we need to see the text or at least have a good idea about its length, format, subject matter and so on before we are able to give the client even a ball-park estimate of the price and deadline.

<u>Before accepting or rejecting a job</u>

Once we have received the text and before accepting the job, we should first study it for terminology and preferably analyse it with our translation software. Note that we should also do this *before rejecting* the text, the reason being that it may be simpler than we first think. For example, a huge text may actually have 90% fuzzy matches (repeated terms and sections or ones you have already translated for a different client). Suddenly, a text that looked impossible within the client's proposed deadline may be possible (even so, in this case we should warn them that this is an exception). It is also necessary to check that the client's word count is correct. If it isn't in Word format, there are lots of word count tools online. Some tools that can help you with this are PractiCount, Count Anything and AnyCount, but if you ask around the translators' forums you'll be sure to find some good advice and preferences.

We may also discover that the format itself is going to be difficult to work with (and thus ask the client for the document in another format or charge them more). And as mentioned before, another nasty surprise may be that the source text itself is badly written and needs correcting before translation. This is a service that should also be paid for.

As we have seen, maybe the client has even sneakily "pre-translated" the document with a machine translator with disastrous results (proper nouns translated, multiple meanings of similar words used out of context, metaphors, word order, calques etc.), expecting you to simply proofread the text and charging less than a translation job. This may happen due to a client's lack of knowledge about what is necessary to do a good translation, assuming that Google is good enough. In this case, we obviously have a duty to the profession to enlighten them. Instead of proofreading such texts, taking longer than translating a well-written text as you use your crystal ball to try to decipher what on earth the author actually meant to say, as I have already suggested you may prefer to have a policy of simply not accepting proofreading or revision work of texts translated by non-native, non-professionals. By letting others do so, we may actually be demeaning and belittling our own profession. Clients need to know that the translation (or any related job) should be left to the professionals.

<u>"You're gonna love this!"</u>

Big advertising agencies always try to create an image in their potential buyers' minds, whether it's a car driving supremely on an empty road or a well-shaven man with a beautiful lady clinging to his smooth jaw. By doing so, they hope to generate a good feeling about their product before the buyer has even bought it, imagining what it will be like when they have it. Like Pavlov's salivating dogs thinking about the next meal, the potential clients are supposedly then ready to buy or commit themselves. *It is not the product, but what the client is going to do with it that entices them to buy it.*

We can do something similar in our own small way with a new client by simply adding a line at the end of our mail such as:

"Sounds like an interesting project; I can't wait to see the translated version on my screen."

"I'm sure this'll look great in the target language [*and will have the desired effect on the readers, whether it's winning a lawsuit, gaining new foreign customers or having a patent passed*]."

Our profession is an odd one in that our clients can never be 100% sure if we have done a good job. (If they could, they would translate the texts or interpret the speech themselves!) For this reason, we have to reassure them of the quality of the product before they even have it, particularly with first-time clients. There are many ways to do this which are mentioned in this book, but keep this fact in mind. The first-time client will always be apprehensive with all that this entails, most notably lots of questions and misconceptions. If you stop to think about it, the first time you pay for the services of a certain lawyer, mechanic, doctor, restaurant or even a hairdresser, you often have a lot of questions simply to check they have understood what you want and they know what they're doing, not because you really want to know the intricate details of their job or even fully understand their answers. It's only natural, so don't panic or get frustrated; just explain things calmly but firmly, answer their queries and above all ask the right questions yourself to allay their fears.

The second time such clients hire your services they should have far fewer doubts and will now trust you more to be able to leave you alone to get on with the job.

Do you really understand the text?

As translators, we are condemned to being cultivated people. We usually win when playing Trivial Pursuit, to the perpetual annoyance of our friends. We are expected to have a far greater vocabulary than other mortals, so we should not be afraid when we see new vocabulary that at first we don't understand. You may surprise yourself in 15 minutes with Wikipedia learning about nuclear power, existentialism or the Cubist movement. Many years ago, I was doing a fairly simple translation about isomers when a translator friend looked at my screen and said she would never be able to translate such a text. I showed her the Wikipedia entry about isomers:

"*In chemistry, **isomers** are compounds with the same molecular formula but different structural formulas. Isomers do not necessarily share similar properties.*"

Is the concept really that difficult? Clearly, we should never translate texts that we do not truly understand; the point I am making is that texts which may at first look difficult may not actually be so hard if you take 30 minutes to check out the terminology and concepts beforehand. I should also stress that Wikipedia is not to be used as reliable reference material! (Google Books can be a relatively reliable terminology source, since the texts appearing there have usually gone through a more meticulous publishing process than the average Wikipedia page.) Nevertheless, it usually gives citations that lead to more reliable sources. Nevertheless, it can be a good learning tool for understanding concepts you are unfamiliar with.

What's in a name?

Then there is the matter of brand names. To illustrate this point, let me tell you an anecdote about the first president of the Republic of Georgia, Eduard Shevardnadze.

One day, he was at the opening of a Coca Cola plant. This was important in creating new jobs in Tiblisi and as a sign of the ex-Soviet Republic's opening to the West. In front of the cameras, he was invited to take a sip of the product for the photo opportunity. He did so, then stepped up to the microphone and announced to the crowd and journalists: "*It tastes like Pepsi!*"

Needless to say, the Coca Cola company was less than impressed. This illustrates the importance of knowing not only about your client company, but also being aware of its rivals. When translating slogans or flagship products, we want to avoid inadvertently using the corporate language typical of rival companies.

It is a universal, unspoken truth that Pepsi and Coke do indeed taste very similar, but it would be corporate suicide for either of the two companies to recognise this fact. If you were translating a text for PepsiCo, for example, you would need to avoid any linguistic references to Fanta products or Powerade, Nestea etc. (Coca Cola products). Similarly, there are household names such as *hoover* that are actually registered company trademarks (which we should refer to as a vacuum cleaner, for example).

A similar consideration needs to be borne in mind when translating new patents. It is very rare for a revolutionary new patent to appear on the market, even if our clients will always claim otherwise when attempting to obtain the patent with your translation. New patents are often simply modifications of existing products. This means that our clients must try to distance themselves from other, similar products already on the market. They may do so by using very different terminology.

Thus, when translating the text, we need to be aware of other similar products' terminology in order to avoid it. We can do so by checking out their websites or at least not using them to find our terminology. Obviously, we can also simply ask our clients for vocabulary they wish to avoid! They should know this information better than anybody.

<u>"Who's going to read it?"</u>

We also need to be aware of the final target readers of the text. What social group do they belong to? Is it a pamphlet to raise awareness about healthcare among the general public or a text that will only be seen by specialist surgeons? Is it for the USA or the UK; Mexico or Spain? As you should know, American English or Spanish can be very different from European English or Spanish. The EU also has specific terminology that even native English speakers may find unfamiliar, intended for communication between non-natives as opposed to just British people.

(Resources here:

http://termcoord.eu/discover/glossaries-by-eu-institutions-and-bodies/

and here:

http://ec.europa.eu/translation/index_en.htm).

Before your text is finally accepted, the company may have the text inexpertly proofread by somebody who spent six months in London and so considers him/herself to be an expert in English, for example. They need to be aware of such subtleties. Try to see the final, published or online text, too, in case such inexpert proofreaders have meddled with the text with catastrophic results.

<u>Asking the client questions</u>

In order to do a good job to the customer's liking, then, it is often essential to ask such questions as those raised above. Inexplicably, there are translators and even agencies that seem to be afraid of asking the client such questions, possibly worrying that they will give the impression that they do not know what they're doing. Nothing could be further from the truth; on the contrary, in fact it is the translator who should be asking questions during the translation process, not the client—provided that we ask the right questions and in the right way, as we shall now see.

When a customer goes into a restaurant and asks for a steak, what's the first thing the waiter always replies? Usually, they say: "How would you like it? (Rare, medium or well-done?)" In other words, the first thing they do is *ask you a question*. The reason they do so is because the chef back in the kitchen is not telepathic. They do not know how the customer prefers their steak. After answering the waiter, the customer can now sit back and relax, knowing that the chef is going to do the job to their liking. Needless to say, we can do the same, as with the checklist we are about to see.

When we go to a mechanic, they also have to ask us questions: "When was your last oil change? What noise is the engine making?" If we go to the doctor, they do the same: "Do you smoke or drink? How much? What did you eat yesterday? Can you describe the pain?" Even a good clothes shop may ask us what occasion we are going to wear the clothes for. When you first enter a clothes shop, the usual question the employees ask you is: "Can I help you?", right? And you usually answer: "I'm just looking," right? This in itself may be a lost sale for the shop, and the reason is because they haven't made the question specific enough to discover the customer's needs. They would do better to ask: "*What are you looking for?* A suit for a wedding, a job interview, or just to look trendy this summer?" Only then will they know what the customer wants and engage their interest.

Clearly, if these service providers don't ask us these questions, it is going to be far more difficult for them to help us and thus do their job well. Far from feeling annoyed at such questions, as customers we feel involved and see that they are taking an interest in our problem. The more pertinent the questions, the more we are reassured on realising that the expert knows what they're doing and is taking the job seriously. If the mechanic doesn't ask questions or look at the engine when giving us the price estimate, it may give the opposite impression. Likewise, a doctor who prescribes us pills without examining us or asking questions will leave us feeling uneasy.

By asking questions you may also discover mistakes in the source text that the client hasn't noticed, as I have done worryingly often when translating contracts ("Do you really mean to say that?" "Shouldn't this sentence be negative?"). This is another service no machine will ever replace, while making you irreplaceable. Remind your client of this when it happens.

Asking the right, intelligent questions can show the client how professional you are and inspire confidence in them as regards your ability to do their job well, taking into account their needs.

<u>"What's it for?"</u>

You can buy a diary for €5, but when you have filled it with your memories it then becomes invaluable. There's a big difference between price, value and *worth*; it is only when the direct client is aware of what your product is *worth* to them that you can seriously demand higher fees from them and they will listen.

The raw material we deal with (the source text) may be valuable in itself to the client, but they may not realise that to maintain its value for the end client (the reader), they need a human professional. The party that creates the text is human (the author) and the party that reads the target text it human (the reader / end client). Therefore, it is only logical that the bridge between those two parties should be a human professional (you), not Google Translate or somebody who translates as a hobby.

In order to help the client realise your product's worth, it is essential to do something that Google Translate can't, which is to ask this question about the text: *"What's if for?"*

Implicit in this question you should find others that appear as you communicate with your potential client (e.g.: *"Who's going to read it?"*, *"Why?"*, *"What's the context?"* etc.), which we shall deal with later in this book.

But never forget to ask *"What's it for?"* if they haven't already told you.

<u>"Training" your clients</u>

As we have seen, we need not be afraid of asking the client relevant questions in order to understand what they really need from their translation and what you need from them in order to do a good job.

The problem for new clients is that they may well be unaware of what is involved in the translation process. We can therefore go a long way to helping the job go smoothly if we "train" them in how to do a good translation.

There are a few good examples we can show clients, such as the American Translators' Association's booklet *Translation: Getting it Right (A guide to buying translation)* which you can download here: http://www.atanet.org/publications/Getting_it_right.pdf. (ASETRAD has published translated versions of this, such as *Todo lo que siempre quiso saber sobre la traducción*, and there is also the original Spanish downloadable pamphlet from La Xarxa, www.xarxativ.es: *¿Por qué necesito un traductor?*, with much input by yours truly.)

These are examples you can show your clients to give them an idea of what's involved in the translation process—and why they should hire you!

Summing up, though, the newbie translation purchaser may need to think about some basic points before even beginning. We could summarize these for them in the form of a checklist to save them and ourselves time.

The client's checklist

Most of the above should be fairly obvious to experienced translators, but we must remember that it may not be at all obvious to our new, monolingual clients. In order to avoid problems half-way through the translation, or even a day before the delivery deadline, we need to clear up such matters with the client well beforehand. Good communication with the client is always necessary and we should never be afraid to ask certain questions for clarification as we have seen, but to avoid annoying a new, busy, first-time translation client unnecessarily, one way of asking these questions may be in the form of a simple questionnaire or checklist. You could send them this along with the budget estimate, for example, leaving it up to them to decide voluntarily if they wish to respond to it. Or else you can prepare a template in the form of an email with these questions, adapting (and reducing) it for each client. Alternatively, you can keep it for your own reference as your own checklist of questions for the client. In any case, you will effectively have warned them in writing and in advance about these potential problems, so they cannot complain if problems then arise precisely because of such matters.

The checklist, then, may look something like this:

1. *Is it translation or interpreting they need?* If it's interpreting, see the brief section on "Small interpreting jobs" (p.255) to form a different checklist.

2. *Does the entire text really need translating?* This question may be particularly relevant if they think your fees are high. For example, are there local, legal or cultural references that may make no sense or be irrelevant for the particular audience? (By saving your client money, you will also gain their trust.)

3. *Is the text completely finished?* Will there be more? How much? Will this text be modified? (If so, wait!)

4. *What is the text for?* Who is the target reader? (Old/young; educated/basic literacy; specialised/general; US/UK/international etc.) Is the style important? Will it require a translator specialising in a particular field? Is the text for internal information purposes, or is it for publication? (In other words, how much does quality matter?)

5. *Would it be better to transcreate than translate?* Particularly with marketing texts, the source text may be completely irrelevant or inappropriate for a different audience (e.g. in a different country). If so, it needs to be re-written from scratch.

6. *Does the company have any material for context and reference?* Might pictures help the translator (and final reader) understand? Does the company have an internal corporate glossary? Would they like one? Is there any vocabulary we should avoid (rival companies and brands)? Should we translate proper nouns? (Give examples from the text if possible.) Does the client have a list of them?

7. *How long will it take?* Think: how long did it take to write the text? How long does it take to read it?

8. *Does the client company have its own in-house proofreader?* Where are they from? USA/UK? Argentina/Spain? Are they qualified or experienced in proofreading?

9. *For revision and proofreading: who (or what) has written or translated the text?* Advise them to write an excellent piece to the best of their abilities in their native language (instead of translating it badly themselves), which you will then translate with all of its linguistic richness. Explain that the result will be far better than simply proofreading a poorly written text. (You could even suggest re-writing an original source text if it's also bad.) It may

also be worth having a different fee for revision and terminology checks (which are actually part of the translation process) than for "just" proofreading.

10. *What is the payment method and terms?* What is the deadline for delivery? Who will pay bank charges, etc.? You may want the client to send you an official purchase order. Get this information in writing, even if it's just an email confirmation.

If you have similar clients due to your specialisations or market niches, you may find certain clients also have other typical complaints or queries that often arise. If this is the case, sit down and prepare a list of these (and possible answers), all neatly written, to save time repeating such matters with new clients from the same sector.

Contact during longer projects

If you have a fairly long project, it is also a good idea to send the client a short update, say once a week, to reassure them for similar reasons. If my mechanic tells me he needs to work on my car for two weeks, I like to know he is actually working on it and not having a beer in the bar next door to the garage. Just let your client know that the project is going to schedule. After your first reading of the text, you should probably have some questions for the client anyhow (internal corporate acronyms or initials, possible mistakes in the source text they will want to be notified of, etc.).

As masters of language, we can also use our client's register to build up a good rapport in our communication with them, without lapsing into linguistic errors, of course.

The cultural adviser

I repeat: don't forget to be your client's cultural consultant, too. In my experience, for example, I have pointed out that their forms translated from Spanish will not need two surname fields in English or that a congress schedule may not be apt for foreign attendees (e.g. lunch at 3 o'clock). Such simple advice as not translating greetings literally may prove vital to clinch a deal. There may even be entire swathes of text that are unnecessary or inappropriate in other countries for legal or cultural reasons. Warn your client before translating them and you will gain their trust.

Indeed, the reason translators as a whole are sometimes lowly paid and viewed as little more than Google Translate is that society and business think we "just translate" words, with little thought for the human intention behind the message. Only when clients realise that translating such cultural nuances is precisely part of our job will they be prepared to pay more for our services. *So get that message out there, and take this into account when marketing your services.*

Email confirmations

One last piece of advice is to always ask for confirmation of receipt when sending your final translated text (or set up automatic confirmation mail)—and wait for that confirmation before switching off your computer or smartphone.

Notifying the client in writing

To sum up, then, don't be afraid to communicate with your client or even to ask questions if you feel there is an ambiguity in the source text (which may even be intentional in legalese, for example), a mistake or simply some possibly corporate jargon that you cannot be expected to know without reading the client's palm, so to speak. In the rare event that the client "doesn't want to be bothered" with questions, you have at least warned them in advance if problems arise from these questions after delivering the text.

Incidentally, to make the client's life easier, when you send them back their source text with comments and questions that you may have after reading it for the first time, try to offer possible solutions that will probably already have occurred to you, so they only have to answer "OK" or "we prefer option B", for example. In addition to making your client's life easier by doing this, you must remember that your client probably does not have the same literary skills as yourself, so they may not even be capable of clearly explaining what they want to say; that's partly what they pay *you* for. In other words, you will save both parties a lot of time and frustration by avoiding lots of emails and annotations back and forth.

<u>When the client doesn't back down</u>

Sometimes the client will strangely insist on using their own preferred terminology. I say *strangely* because they are paying you precisely because you are the expert. It's a little like a car mechanic advising you to change the air filter, to which you reply, "No, actually I'm rather fond of that filter; I'd rather keep it." Or refusing the doctor's prescribed pills because you don't like their taste. But for some reason, possibly due to the general lack of knowledge about our profession and the fact that many people think they master a language more than they really do, once in a while you will find a customer who insists on using a particular word or expression, even though you know that it will be a disaster in the target country. (Curiously, in my experience this often happens with clients from the world of advertising and marketing, who should be very aware of the importance of globalisation and localisation experts such as ourselves, with the possibly catastrophic effects of not heeding our advice.)

What should we do in this situation? Well, as in the case of a mechanic's advice about replacement parts or a doctor's prescription, in the end it is the client's choice as to whether or not they accept the professional's opinion and go ahead.

Of course we should be cautious, above all in fields that may not be our precise specialisations. There's a big difference between *food safety* and *food security*, for instance. At first sight, such expressions may seem to be wrong if it's not your field, so always check. There may even be brand names etc. we are not aware of.

Also, if your client's complaint is very general and you disagree, ask for specific examples at least so you can reply. Perhaps their internal proofreader is not a native professional or have "over-corrected", replacing your lexis with synonyms. You may even suggest or provide an opinion from an independent party such as a colleague you know.

Style guides can also back you up. In English I prefer *New Hart's Rules* and *The Economist Style Guide*, but avoid *The Guardian*'s. You should be using such guides anyhow.

But if you are totally sure of your terminology, context and sources, never forget that *you* are the linguistic professional, not the client. Of course, if we are certain about the client's mistake and that it may have disastrous consequences (for example in medical or legal texts), we should warn them in writing.

Imagine you go to your family doctor and ask if it would be OK to stop taking your prescribed pills for a couple of days the next weekend for some reason. The doctor could say, "Sure, do whatever you like," or "No way; you can't skip a single one, for these reasons..." Which answer will inspire more confidence and trust in you as a patient/client? You may not like to hear that you can't do whatever you like, but the professional who is insistent and gives reasons inspires more trust because we see they are certain they know what they are doing. A professional who simply says "yes" to everything that the client requests without presenting arguments does not.

When all is said and done, however, the final text is the client's property (once they have paid for it). As such, they can do with it as they wish. A restaurant customer is free to put ketchup on their caviar if they like.

Back to our local mechanic once again. Whenever they change a part in your car, they usually keep the replaced, broken part for you to see it and give you a verbal explanation of what they have done. They probably know we have little idea of what they're talking about, but they do it anyway. Why?

The reason is to gain our confidence. Firstly, we need to see the replaced part to be sure they have truly replaced it, since we often can't see the part from the outside of the car and haven't seen them working on it. *To gain a client's confidence, it is not enough to do a good job; they must see and understand that you have done a good job.* We can also see that the replaced car part is truly broken. Moreover, it is a chance for the mechanic to impress us with their professional knowledge and make us feel involved in the job, as well as informing us about the current state of our car following the repairs. Similarly, we can give a brief explanation of the criteria we have used in our translation or review and the reasons why. For example, I might tell a Spanish client that I have translated *presidente* as *prime minister*, not *president*, since Spain is a parliamentary monarchy, not a republic. They may not be at all interested in this information, but they *are* interested in seeing that I pay attention to such things and know my specialisations. (They may even be able to impress their friends and clients with these snippets of professional knowledge!)

Mechanics can also give us some advice for the future handling and care of our car, acting as our mechanical consultant as well as a mere mechanical repair provider. I remember going to a mechanic when I lived in a different city to check up on my recently bought new car who advised me to drive a little more slowly to improve fuel consumption, thereby saving me about €40 a month. Such advice, like the shop assistant's, costs the mechanic nothing and takes only a few seconds of their time, yet the effect of this little extra service on the customer's confidence is priceless. We can do something similar. On sending the final text to a new client, we may point out information we have come across in the internet while doing the job that may be useful to them, or suggest specific terminology they could use in future with their end clients, how to greet them in emails, etc. We could even hand over a glossary we have drawn up while doing the job. Let them know you are building up a glossary of their specific terminology anyhow, as this is another reason for them to continue hiring you.

My mechanic also complains about his back problems and how much effort the job took him, but I don't advise whining to your clients about your wrist tendinitis!

The grocer's last words

All greengrocers in markets around the world have a final question for their customers just before taking their money: "Anything else?"

They may even make suggestions about a special offer. Supermarkets do something similar by displaying impulse-purchase products such as special discounts and sweets at loud toddlers' eye-level at the checkout. They also place essential items such as bread far from the checkout so that customers have to pass by lots of other tempting products before they reach what they actually came in for. Have you ever been to a supermarket and only bought a loaf of bread? Probably not. Psychologists know that this is because once we have decided to buy something, our mental "floodgates" have opened us up to the idea of spending money, so forking out a little more on an item we hadn't considered before doesn't seem so bad as when we are first offered the same product separately. If you're buying skis, why not buy ski gloves, too?

We can do something similar by reminding our clients of our availability, particularly if we have noticed in the text that there will be other related texts forthcoming. Perhaps you could even suggest a useful job such as writing a standard template email for their foreign clients if you see they have trouble with this (even in their native language you could suggest a native colleague prepare one for them). In any case, if it is an important client it is worth mentioning that you are available for free, simple linguistic or cultural queries in future, so they will keep your address on file and come back to you.

By way of example, I once went to a mechanic because my car's headlights needed adjusting before my motor ordinance test. It was a simple job that took him five minutes and he waived the fee as a sign of goodwill. I thanked him and left to wash the car before the test. However, on washing the car I noticed that the tread on the tyres was wearing a little thin, so I decided I should buy a new set. Guess where I went to buy them, eventually spending over €200? Right; straight back to the same mechanic who had showed me such honesty and goodwill. He had won over a new client.

Meddling customers

After handing in the final text, ask to see the final product if it's going to appear on a website or in a magazine, etc. The reason for this is that on publishing it, a graphic designer may have decided that a comma didn't look very nice, for example, with unfortunate results. There may even be inappropriate side texts or pictures that you were unaware of and which may have a terrible effect when placed alongside the translated text. (e.g.: http://read.bi/1EBU1Va).

<u>What if I see a mistake too late?</u>

If the final text has already been published and you spot a mistake that has slipped past your proofreader (or the client's/agency's proofreader), what should you do?

Well, what would you want the restaurant to do if they discover they have just served up yesterday's fish by mistake? Or the mechanic forgot to screw a bolt back on? Obviously, we would want them to tell us as soon as possible. We can also do so and offer a discount. This can even have a positive effect by showing the client that you are honest. We may still go back to a restaurant if we know that they will tell us about any mistakes made in the kitchen and correct them, as opposed to one where we don't feel well after dining and remain suspicious.[11]

---

[11] Please note that my examples of mechanics, restaurants and grocers are used as examples that we can all relate to. In fact, translators should really compare themselves to doctors, engineers and architects, particularly in terms of income. That said, there will always be a wide range of incomes and top-end clients to seek out in any profession. I imagine that Lady Gaga's hairdresser does not charge $20 a session. The French President Hollande was revealed to be paying his personal hairdresser about €10,000 a month (*The Guardian*, 13 July, 2016).

Is the customer always right?

As we saw before, sometimes a customer may insist on making a linguistic mistake or even doing something with the text that you disagree with for whatever reason. If this is the case, you may want to ask them not to publish your name as the translator, disowning the text. This is not usually a problem; in fact, the problem is usually quite the opposite: getting your name recognised.

After warning them in writing if necessary, we should let the final product go to its rightful owner: the buyer.

In other words:

*The customer is **not** always right, but the customer always **has** the right.*

Organising Your Freelance Life

In all walks of life we have to juggle many commitments: fix that flashing light on the car dashboard, plan our holidays, see the kids' soccer match, answer those emails (social and work-related), tidy those shelves, walk the dog, get regular exercise, and even those "some day" wishes such as visiting the Grand Canyon, learning to bake a great sponge cake or studying something for pleasure.

Equally in all walks of life, this mental juggling act stresses out even the greatest of minds, and more so if you are your own boss. The main reason it stresses us out so much is because we have it all in our heads and not in any particular, logical order. While working on a text for a deadline today, you may get an email about a big translation from a good, loyal client or a domestic emergency that will need attending to later in the day. As you work through the text, these niggling thoughts at the back of your mind may distract you since you know you mustn't forget about them and you'll have to deal with them at some point, not to mention those "some day" projects such as learning how to play the harp that you just don't ever seem to find the time for and end up worrying about at night. Let's look at some tips to tackle this mental conundrum simply and smooth out our organisation.

<u>Writing it down</u>

Long before digital tablets came out, the first tablets were made of clay in the Bronze Age, yet their basic function was not so different from those of today: to organise the owner's life. They were used to write down how much wheat or cattle belonged to different people, for recording events or giving instructions. The reason for this, obviously, was because as civilisation became more complex it became too difficult to keep all of this information in people's heads. Indeed, the very need to record information is how writing itself began. The same principle applies today and we should never forget it: the first step to reduce stress from information overload is simple: *write it down*. Get it out of your head and onto your computer, phone or paper, whatever suits you best.

Having said this, of course we don't want to have lots of lists or Post-Its® lying around, either. We have to write it down in an orderly way for it to be truly useful and remembered; yet simply, too, so it doesn't require much effort.

Let's look at how to do so.

Lists

The good old shopping list is also a very old information tool that we still use today, and little wonder. If we break down a shopping list, we can see it is a deceptively simply data gathering and processing file. We can also see why it's so useful and apply it to other areas of our lives.

If you still use a paper shopping list, where do you keep it? The best bet is in your kitchen, most probably on the fridge door. Why? Clearly, because it is precisely when we are in the kitchen or looking in the fridge that we will realise what we need to put on the list, so it's the perfect place to gather the data. In other words, we keep the list in a place where it'll be useful to us, then take it with us to the other place where it'll be useful to us to process the data: the shop, in this case.

Our list, then, needs to be handy to be used in the appropriate location. But of course, we may find that we need more washing powder when the laundry in the basement needs doing or simply remember something while we're out in the street. If we have the list in a booklet in our pocket or better still on our smartphone connected to our other devices, instead of on the fridge door, then we can update it immediately wherever and whenever appropriate. But why not do this with other lists?

In other words, the good old shopping list is an example of a "place list", to be used in a specific place. We can apply this principle to any other place we wish.

Place lists

The next time you go to your city centre or even your office or home, it may be useful to have a list of things you can deal with when you're there all on one list, which you can add to whenever anything useful occurs to you. Then, the next time you go to the city centre, you can do everything at once (make an enquiry at your bank in person, post that parcel at the Post Office, etc.).

People lists

The same applies to people. If there are significant people in your life (spouse, friend, accountant (!), etc.), it may be an idea to have a file for each person so you don't forget everything you have to say or deal with next time you see them or bump into them. It may seem a very cold way of dealing with some human relationships, but it's much better than forgetting those Valentine's' Day or anniversary arrangements (!). And if you have it all on your smartphone, it's very easy to check anyhow.

Low energy lists

Another practical list you may consider using is a "low energy" list.

Just as we can list all those things that can only be done at a certain location or with a particular person, we can also list those mundane jobs that you don't really feel like doing but which require little mental effort (such as testing the air in your car's tyres, tidying your office space or cupboards, sorting out the business cards or CVs you've received at a congress or via email, etc.). When work is slow but you don't feel particularly energetic or it's a rainy weekend, now is the time to whip out the "low energy" list and go through it.

Grouping tasks

The idea of making simple lists really boils down to grouping tasks we have to do into more manageable chunks instead of spreading them out over time and space so that they become unwieldy. We can essentially group any tasks we have to do, such as making phone calls or emails, and do them all together at the same time.

Organising email

Now let's look at your email. As you work, you will probably get emails that need to be answered or acted upon the same day (ideally, you should be checking your mail hourly so as not to miss important job offers etc.). All of our incoming mail falls into five basic categories, which we can call:

i)   2-minute mail;

ii)   Doable;

iii)   Pending;

iv)   Reference;

v)   Trash.

Let's look at the first type, where we can apply the two-minute rule: **if it can be dealt with or answered in two minutes, do it** *now*. Don't let it nag you at the back of your mind for the rest of the day. (Note that the two-minute rule can apply to anything in life that will take this long: hang up that jacket, clean that coffee cup, etc., so as not to let little jobs pile up.)

If it will take more than two minutes, we have two options: decide if we can also still do it now anyway, or label/file it. (In Gmail, it is very simple to create files for mail with one click, and even easier to simply label and unlabel it. If you don't have a Gmail account, you may wish to set one up and redirect mail from your main address there, if only for the sake of organisation. This will also give you access to a great many other easily connected Google-related time savers such as Drive, Keep, Boomerang, the interactive calendar, etc.)

If the mail needs an answer or action from us, then we can label it "Doable", for example. Then, when we next check our mail, we can check all of the "Doable" mail at one sitting, and decide which ones we can or must answer in the time we have available. As we work on our translations, we can now relax in the knowledge that we haven't forgotten about those mails and they won't be festering at the back of our mind.

The other important file/label you should have is the "Pending/Waiting" one. This applies to mail that will require a reply or action from *other* people, or which can't be acted upon by us until a certain date or event has taken place (e.g. tax returns). (Incidentally, for mail requiring action after a certain date we should also put a reminder on our calendars. If you come across something interesting for a future date in the internet and don't have time to take down the details, check out Cloquo.com to get reminders.) Immediately after (or just before) sending any email, even if it is only a short, two-minute one, we should decide if it will require a reply from the addressee or if the thread is now finished. If it will need a reply, then clearly it gets labelled/filed as "Pending/Waiting" or suchlike. Once in a while—maybe only once a week—you can check these mails to see if those addressees have got back to you or not.

Don't forget to unlabel mails when their labels no longer apply! If not, they may build up and you'll be back to the original problem of sifting through your mail to see what needs answering etc.

Then there are the mails that may provide us with information that may be useful some day (e.g. general information from your accountant about new government laws that may affect you if you earn more this year). We can have a general "Reference" label or file for these mails, or perhaps more specific ones (e.g. "Tax info", "Congresses next year", etc.).

And finally, of course, there is junk mail. Be ruthless. If you're sure an email is of no use to you, bin it. Don't let it clutter up your mail.

If you feel you need to take your email organisation to another level, perhaps for a marketing drive or simply because you are having to process a huge volume, check out Xobni, which can also help control your social networks in general.

Project micro-management

What is a project?

For the purpose of organisation (not just translation projects), we can consider a project to be *anything that requires more than one action*. Whether it's visiting Machu Pichu or getting a new spare tyre for your car, if it involves more than one step then it's worth getting organised, and that means first writing it down. But don't panic; in any project there is actually extremely little that we actually need to write down, as we shall now see.

It should be remembered that any project, big or small, needs a decision to be taken about what the next physical or actionable step actually is. So you want to visit the Grand Canyon? It is not enough to simply write in a "Some Day" list or file something vague like "Visit the Grand Canyon". Have you actually thought about what is necessary? Flights? A visa for the USA? On writing down the first practical step, you are on the path to achieving that goal.

"A journey of a thousand miles begins with a single step."

Laozi

The above statement is very true, which is why we need to identify that first step to be able to begin any journey or project.

I would also add: *"The most important step is always the **next one**—so write it down!"*

And for longer projects:

"*'Some day'* never comes until you give it a date."

Gary Smith ☺

Juggling lots of things to do in your head causes unnecessary stress and mistakes. Tired western hikers in the Himalayas with all the latest clothes and equipment are often surprised to see local monks in sandals happily making their pilgrimages seemingly effortlessly. The reason may be because, whereas the holiday hikers are only thinking about their destination miles and weeks ahead, the monks are simply enjoying and contemplating the next simple step.

It is psychologically much easier to concentrate on this than on the entire project.

Doable or Pending?

The simple method we have discussed of "Doable" emails (i.e. ones you should reply to) and "Pending" emails (i.e. awaiting a reply from others or a specific date) can actually be applied to your work and in fact all of the projects, big or small, you have in life.

You can set up a folder for each project, or a simple word document with a table of two columns entitled "Pending/Waiting" (for others to act or for specific dates and places you often go to) and "Doable" (for you to act on yourself). Usually, you will only use one column at a time for each mini project, and you only need to write one thing there: the next action/step.

For example, let's say you have to get a new spare tyre for your car before you go away next weekend. The first and most important step in any project, however big, small, vague or detailed, is to **decide what the first step is**.

So let's see:

Do you know the size of your car's tyres? If you don't remember, you'll have to find this information (maybe it's in the manual in the car's glove compartment in a garage or in the street). So this is the first step. (We can even now add or connect this action to a place list such as "Car" or "Street", or simply add the location to the same note, as below.)

Project: Get new spare tyre (Step 1)

Doable   *Pending*

Find out tyre size. (Street)

Now we've written the first/next step down, we can leave the project here and come back to it later if necessary (or simply do it now, move on to the next step and write that one down instead if you are interrupted then). Once we've done the action (finding the tyre size), we can then delete the action and maybe write the relevant information (the tyre size) in the same column or in an attached reference list/file to help with the next step (getting the tyre), which you can now write down. But do you know where to get the tyre? If not, you may have to check the prices and places on the internet. This will be our next step, then, so again we write it down in the "Doable" column:

Project: Get new spare tyre (Step 2)

Doable   *Pending*

Find tyre dealer.

(Internet?)

(Size: xxx)

When you get a moment, you can do exactly this without worrying about this little project for the rest of the day.

When you find the right tyre dealer and call them, maybe they don't know if they have your tyre in stock; they say they'll get back to you. Now you can delete "Find tyre dealer" from the "Doables" column and write in the "Pending" column opposite, something like:

Project: Get new spare tyre (Step 3)

Doable   *Pending*

                                      Waiting for reply from dealer (Phone no.: 555...)

Any useful information to carry out the next step should be written down (such as the phone no. here). Indeed, if we are interrupted while doing a task, we should *write down the last thing we were doing* (or were about to do) so we can return to it and start again where we left off.

In this case, when the dealer finally replies, you will then either need to go and buy the tyre or call another dealer. So, we now delete the item from the "Pending/Waiting" column and write the next step in the "Doables" column. And so on until the project is completed.

Remember that you *only have to write down the next step if you are interrupted* at any time, for example to do an urgent translation. Then you can relax by simply closing the project and attend to the interruption, safe in the knowledge that afterwards you can turn back to this table and hit the ground running, continuing the project without missing a beat trying to remember what you had to do next. *If there are no interruptions during a small project such as changing a spare tyre, you may not need to write any step down or use the project table at all; just continue until you finish the whole project.*

The great thing about this system is its simplicity: you only need to think about one thing at a time. In fact, you don't even have to think about it, because it's written down for you to look at when you get a moment. This simple act of taking something out of your head and putting it on paper or a computer file can be a great psychological relief.

The Reference file

Another useful file to have for each project (as well as the Doable/Pending list) is a Reference file. Here you can jot down any ideas that come to you while watching T.V., having lunch or meditating, so they don't get forgotten. On the internet you can use pages such as Pocket (for websites) or Pinterest privately for a similar effect. Again, a smartphone is an excellent tool here, especially if you connect it to Google Drive or a Dropbox account, for example, so that it will immediately appear on your laptop, home computer or tablet, too. Tools such as Evernote and Google Keep can also greatly aid you.

The bigger picture

Another important factor when we have to juggle many tasks in our day-to-day lives is prioritising. If you have trouble doing this, it may be wise to set aside an hour or two every week to review your files and set out some priorities for the coming days so that you don't have to do so every time you look at your files. I find a good time for this is on Monday mornings before the translation work begins to come in. Project managers or agencies may prefer Friday around noon before everybody leaves, so that everyone knows what they have to do when they come back on Monday and can hit the ground running. The important point is to prioritise if necessary once in a while so you don't have to worry about it all the time. Remember, too, to use calendar reminders for things that cannot be delayed or can only be done after a certain date (e.g. early bird offers for congresses) so you keep certain actions in mind when prioritising. And I repeat, a calendar synced with your smartphone and PC works wonders (e.g. a Google account, iCloud, etc.).

For those bigger projects in life, we need to take time to brainstorm or simply see the forest instead of the trees (we may realise we're not even in the right forest!). This does not mean day-dreaming or being inefficient. It is simply another, higher level of organisation and we must find time for it if we are going to get round to doing new projects.

"A goal without a plan is just a wish."

Saint-Exupery

<u>Prioritising</u>

Psychologists have shown us that it is tempting and deceptively satisfying to do smaller, less important jobs first, but often this is simply procrastination, putting off the bigger, more important ones. As in medical triage, we should do the latter first. Even if we have two weeks to do a translation that will probably only take us one, we should try to do it first, perhaps dividing it up into manageable, measurable chunks (e.g. a certain amount of words) over a few days. Other tasks, jobs and emergencies may crop up over the week, making the bigger, more significant job more urgent and stressful to finish if you've been putting it off to do smaller, less urgent tasks.

<u>Clutter</u>

What about your workspace? Is it cluttered? If so, you need an inbox and an outbox, just like your email. Go through *everything* that is bugging you: those holiday brochures you were going to look at, those papers and notes taken at a congress two years ago that you didn't get round to looking at, etc. Round them all up and literally put them in a basket if necessary so you can go through them on a rainy weekend or a slow work day (as with your low energy list). If there are non-physical items that need addressing or ones that don't fit in the basket, such as that flickering room light, the shelf that needs fixing, etc., then note them down in a "Home" or "Office" list with the first step written in the "Doables" column. (You can literally put such a paper list in said basket, too.)

Some people with large families even have little baskets for each member of the family in which to drop reminders or simply things they've left lying around the house!

For general household or office organisational tips and encouragement, checkout www.UnfuckYourHabit.com.

<u>Do, Date, Delegate or Dump</u>

Finally, there may come a time when, even though you are perfectly organised, you simply find you don't humanly have enough time to do everything you have before you. If this is the case, you may simply have taken on more than you can do, biting off more than you can chew. What can we do about this? Well, there are four basic options for each item: *Do, Date, Delegate or Dump*.

Do: Decide to do it now (or this week, etc.) to get it off your *To Do* list, rather like the 2-minute rule.

Date: Put a later date on it. In other words, rearrange it. This may mean renegotiating with a client or simply with yourself, maybe putting it on the backburner in a "Projects" file or shifting it to a later date in your calendar. Note: this does not mean procrastinating. When you see that date approaching, get ready.

Delegate: Delegate it in somebody else. Pay a professional, and I'm not just talking about translation here. Maybe you could pay somebody to clean your house, for example. You may find that a professional will take two hours a week to do a better job than you can do in four hours, and in those two hours you can earn more than enough to pay them. It makes economic and practical sense. You can also find virtual assistants and secretaries in countries with cheaper economies to do specific time-consuming secretarial work or email campaigns, for example (e.g. AskSunday.com, elance.com, TasksEveryDay.com and YourManInIndia.com).

Dump: Decide *not* to do it, if this is possible, and delete it. In the end, however well organised we may be, we are only human and we sometimes need to take a conscious decision to let some things go. Once you have had a good think about it and taken this decision, relax and forget about it.

Let's look a practical example of applying this system. Imagine your white-walled office is looking a little grey and needs painting. If work is slack, you may decide to buy some paint and brushes and get to work (*Do*). If not, you can put aside a couple of days, maybe even a weekend, to do it (*Date*). Or else you could put your faith in a professional (*Delegate*)—which is probably wiser (!), though you'll still need to set a date, too. Or finally, if you work alone, nobody actually visits your office and it really doesn't bother you, then you may simply decide that it's not an important priority for you and forget all about it for another year or two (*Dump*).

The point about making such decisions is that once you have written it down or simply dumped the whole idea, you can and should take the weight of responsibility off your mind. This is essential for the mental health of the freelance translator.

<u>Time is money</u>

Clearly, one of the great advantages of freelance translation is that technically you can work almost anywhere, anytime you like. Nevertheless, if you are a disaster at administering your own time, you will rarely be able to take advantage of this wonderful perk. Time lost can indeed mean money lost, so we need to learn how to make the most of it.

One obvious danger is found in the social networks themselves, even though these should also be part of our job in terms of marketing ourselves. It's all too easy to fall into the black hole of Facebook and Twitter. A five minute break becomes half an hour—which you will have to make up for later—as you get involved with a discussion in a translators' forum or looking at your friend's holiday photos. One trick to help avoid this is the now famous pomodoro technique. This involves using a timer with an alarm to give yourself just a five-minute break after twenty-five minutes of work, for example. (You can download or use freeware with alarms online (e.g. tomato-timer.com) or which tell you to get back to work or only allow you to access Facebook at certain times, if you need such disciplining.) It is usually more productive to work in two twenty-five minute stints per hour for three hours than to work for two or three hours with a half-hour break. A two-and-a-half-hour translation slog in front of the computer will leave you feeling tired and losing concentration. Short breaks are more effective in keeping you alert. If you drink coffee immediately before taking a 20-minute nap (by which time the caffeine is beginning to kick in), you should wake up feeling alert instead of groggy, too.

Simply putting limits on your work time (and entire working day) can improve your productivity in that time a great deal. There are some useful tools on the internet to help you manage your time more effectively. As mentioned above, Hootsuite enables you to send out Tweets and posts on Facebook and LinkedIn on the day and at the time of your choice. This means you can plan a good internet presence when you need it. You may decide to post a useful article just when people are waking up on the West Coast of the USA while you're fast asleep in London. Having said that, if you live in Los Angeles you may want to send a job at EOB (End Of Business), say around 5 p.m. local time, to a colleague who is just waking up in New Zealand. Likewise, they can send you the finished job or comments when they're switching off and you're switching on. Take advantage of our global profession and tools!

There are also downloadable tools that record how long you spend on Facebook etc. every day, so you can see where you are "wasting" your time (e.g. www.RescueTime.com).

Different people also seem to have different times of day when they work best. If you have family commitments or are travelling, this may dictate your working hours, but most people seem to function best in the morning. Some also prefer to burn the midnight oil with the peace that night time brings. Others even work best with six hours' sleep at night and two in the afternoon. Do whatever suits you best; you could even try different timetables for a few weeks until you find the one that works for you.

Organising your time in general will leave you more free time in general, too, so take it seriously. Apply the two-minute rule: if you can do it in two minutes, do it now; don't put it to the back of the list to nag at the back of your mind for the rest of the day. And if not, remember to note it down as doable or pending, perhaps simply on a Windows notepad you can keep in a corner of your screen.

It is a fact that if you are given a tight deadline you'll work much more intensely than if you have all day to translate a short, simple text. So give yourself a deadline, even for a short text the client has given you plenty of time to translate. Don't let the job drag on unnecessarily.

Another factor that may affect your time usage greatly on a much bigger scale is simply the kind of client or job that wastes your time unnecessarily with constant little demands, whether this is due to the text format, your client's methods of work or the type of text itself. As well as keeping track of how much you earn from each client over the year on an Excel sheet, it is an idea to clock how much time you spend with each client, too. This way, you can truly know how much you are actually earning per hour with each one. The 80/20 rule or "Pareto principle" is now generally accepted in business. What this means for you is that it is quite possible that 80% of your income per hour comes from just 20% of your clients—and vice versa. Clearly, you need to take time to sit down and discover who those clients are that are bringing in 80% of your income but only taking up 20% of your time. Once in a while, we need to take stock of the bigger picture in this respect to re-orient our business and its goals.

<u>Systems</u>

Creating a timetable for your average working day not only helps you; it also helps your clients. As in any successful franchise system, customers like to get the feel of having a similar experience every time they use the service as it gives them a sense of security that things are being done well according to an organised plan. At first they may not like the fact that you don't work after 7 p.m., but when they get used to it they know when you're available and when you're not, except in emergencies.

The same goes for your way of working with each client, the questions (or check list) you put to them, your invoice's format and even your branding if you wish to create a logo, etc. When they get used to your way of working it becomes uncomfortable for them to change to another service provider.

<u>Growing your business</u>

If freelancing isn't enough and you have a desire for world domination or to set up a small company, it is necessary to put the "skeleton" of your business in place before fleshing it out as your business grows.

In any case, you may find that the busier you become, the more different tasks unrelated to translation you have: accountancy, marketing, etc. If you don't have some kind of structure in place to deal with this, it may become a problem even as a lone freelancer. If you intend to set up a business with employees or partners, this could spell disaster as your jobs and responsibilities begin to overlap, with people blaming others when things get neglected or done badly due to everybody multitasking.

So, if you intend to set up a growing business or company, first sit down and think of all the freelancing tasks you already do: writing out invoices, different forms of marketing, etc. (You may also wish to break down the entire translation process as a project manager would do, from looking at the text to see if it falls within your skills (or those of your team or colleagues), correspondence with incoming clients, translation, revision, proofreading, reviewing, dealing with clients' and translators' queries, etc.). Although as a freelancer you are already doing all of these tasks yourself, write each of them out as if it were a job description, as if your freelance business were 1,000 times bigger and thus you need somebody in each of those tasks to do a full-time job in each. As your business grows, you'll find that some of these tasks do indeed take up too much of your time and you will need to outsource them—or find an employee for them. Since you already have the job description that you know needs covering, then you know exactly what jobs you simply need to outsource and can tell your new colleagues/helpers/employees what to do, avoiding overlapping responsibilities.

Of course, as we have already seen, you may simply decide to hunt for better customers and hence better fees, honing your skills and specialisations and thus keeping your business small but growing your personal income with more or less the same amount of work. You can still make a good living as a freelancer!

Where to work

Freelance translation also allows us to work wherever we like. I myself live next to a Mediterranean beach and have sometimes found it tempting to have a coffee on a terrace by the sand while working, sometimes gloating by posting pics of the situation on the social networks. However, I've found that by mixing work and play in this way, you actually end up being a little distracted when you should be working, while not really relaxing because you have to work. It's better to work in a working environment where you concentrate best with a set timetable and time limit, then go and truly relax with that coffee on the beach to the full with no worries about work while you're there.

This clearly applies to nomad translators. Translation is indeed a profession by which you can (and perhaps sometimes should) travel and work. However, if you are going to do so try to make sure that wherever you are you have some kind of workable space where you can concentrate without distractions and dedicate a few hours a day completely to your work.

Some translators also find that hiring a coworking office space helps them get into the right frame of mind for working, being surrounded by other freelancers concentrating hard on their work. It can also lead to some useful business contacts.

It is a running joke that translators are hermits that work at home in their pyjamas. While it is often a great advantage to work from home, we shouldn't let this poor example become a way of life. Create some kind of routine, have a shower, get out at least once a day and talk to real people before you start losing touch with reality!

Different translators work better under different conditions. Some prefer to work all night in darkness, some with music in the background (personally, I don't like either of these). Clearly, whatever helps your mental agility is good for you. And while we do not need such a great level of physical agility as mental agility, our job does indeed entail very real physical risks that we must attend to. We shall now look at some tips on how to do so.[12]

---

[12] If you have found the tips in this section useful, I also recommend David Allen's book, *Getting Things Done*, which gives a wealth of advice on organisation. There is even an app based on it called *Chaos Control*.

The Translator's Health

Ergonomics

Believe it or not, translation can be a dangerous job. Holding the same awkward position for many hours can cause musculoskeletal, tendon and nerve disorders leading to chronic pain and stiffness in the back, neck, shoulders and wrists, not to mention the effects of repetitive finger movements and localised pressure. Dealing with these problems is not just a question of your own health; the more comfortable you are, the longer you can work and make money!

Some translators use voice recognition software such as Dragon (www.nuance.com/dragon) to avoid such problems, though they will still have to be sitting in front of the screen most of the time.

Let's take a look first at how your workspace should be arranged to avoid these problems.

The chair

First, the chair. As your backside will be parked here for many hours a week, not to mention throughout your working life, it is clearly worth forking out a little cash to make sure this is comfortable. The essential features are:

-    A cushion underneath you. This sounds pretty obvious; a hard chair is obviously not a comfortable place to spend eight hours a day.

-    A cushion tucked behind your lower back. If your chair does not have an adjustable back rest (as it should), then you should really place a cushion or rolled-up towel here. Our spine naturally curves slightly outwards, but without this support you will find it gradually curving inwards (i.e. you will start hunching over your screen and keyboard) with all of the back problems this entails.

-    Adjustable seat height. This is necessary so that you can position yourself comfortably in front of the screen, keyboard and desk at a height that lets you sit easily with a straight back and no need to crane yourself forward.

-    The chair should also be able to swivel round, so you're not twisting and straining entirely with your hands and arms every time you reach for something.

-    Your chair should ideally have arm rests, again to avoid straining this part of your body by holding them aloft for hours at a time in the same position.

-    I have also found it helpful to sit on a fitball sometimes while working to improve my posture.

The keyboard

As for the keyboard, I have found the best kind to be those which have a pad on which to rest your palms instead of having to hold your hands in the air like a pianist, especially when not typing. You may be able to make yourself such a makeshift pad, but the Logitech Wave keyboard I use works fine, for example. I would also recommend this keyboard because its shape is slightly curved so that your hands are pointing a little inwards in a natural position as opposed to jutting out from your body at right angles. It also has little props so that it's inclined a little towards the user, which is also more comfortable, though you can create the same effect by propping your keyboard up a little with a book, for example. If your desk has a sliding keyboard tray beneath the desktop, use it. It is there so that your hands are in a naturally more relaxed position instead of raising your hands above your elbows. Ideally, your elbow angles should be about 90° between forearm and upper arm, and your keyboard at about 60° from your horizontal line of vision.

Try to use hotkeys and keyboard shortcuts with the Ctrl key (e.g. http://ow.ly/HQ5Fd) to avoid reaching for the mouse every ten seconds, too, especially for the most basic commands that you use all the time. This will also improve your speed considerably and I strongly advise using them, especially for basic, repetitive operations (e.g. select (Shift+Ctrl+arrows), copy (Ctrl+c) and paste (Ctrl+v)). If you must use a mouse, make sure it is as near to your keyboard as possible to avoid the same, unnecessary repeated stretching movement.

The screen

Now the screen. The top of your screen should be at about the height of your eyes, so that you are actually looking slightly downwards at it. It should also be tilted slightly backwards (20°-30° from the vertical). Your face/eyes should be further than 40 cm and closer than 1 m from the screen, without your head craning forward. Try to buy a screen with an independent base that lets you tilt and turn it as you like.

It is also useful to use a grey background on your screen while working so as to avoid the white glare that can cause eye strain. (More specifically, the most comfortable colours are: black characters on a white or yellow background; yellow on black, white on black; white on blue; and green on white. Try them out and see which you prefer. Red, green and yellow on white are the worst colours for comfortable vision, though some clients don't seem to appreciate this!) The essential point for clarity is that there should be a good contrast between the text and the background.

Keep the brightness down to a comfortable level anyhow. The best kind of screen to avoid glare is an LCD screen, though you may find it causes reflections. In any case, these days LED screens are usually quite comfortable for one's eyesight. Avoid CRT screens, especially below 75 Hz, which cause flicker. When buying, try adjusting the brightness and looking at it from various angles to see if you can see what's on the screen comfortably. The bigger the screen, the better. Matte screens are better than shiny ones for your eyesight, too (you can buy a matte screen protector if yours is shiny), and a black frame is preferable.

I also use a curious free application called *f.lux* (https://justgetflux.com). This turns the blues of your screen off as the sun goes down in your part of the world. The theory behind this is that our computer screens (and mobile devices) use a lot of light similar to natural daylight, which means that if we're working long after sunset our brain is still telling us that it's still daytime because of the light we're receiving as we stare at the screen. With this little app, the screen gradually turns a pleasant shade of orange as daylight disappears outside. (In general, it's better to use "warm" colour (reds and yellows) for weak light, and "cool" ones (greens and blues) for strong light.) I find that it does actually work, so that when I go to bed I still feel naturally tired and ready for sleep. (Of course, if you've accepted an all-night rush job and need to burn the midnight oil, you'd better shut it off!) If you don't have a blue filter option on your mobile phone, avoid using it around bedtime, too, and keep its brightness down when indoors to save your battery and eyesight.

In any case, artificial lighting in your room should be over 30° from your line of sight and not shining directly down on your desktop, either, but at about 45° if possible.

When working, also try to look away from the screen from time to time, preferably outside into the distance, so that your eyes still get some exercise focussing on different distances. Changing your posture so that your eye-to-screen distance varies from time to time also helps. Any bright light sources, whether natural or artificial, should not be near the screen or reflecting off it, but rather to the side of you. As a general rule, ambient light should be similar in intensity to the light from your screen.

Finally, you may find it helpful to use more than one screen to avoid constantly toggling between tasks on the same one.

The mouse

If you really must use a mouse, make sure your wrist is not making a right angle. Preferably, it should be resting on a surface with your hand and forearm forming a more or less straight line.

Feet

You should also have a footrest. There are professional ones you can buy, but just about anything will do. The important thing is that your feet should not be dangling straight down to the floor but resting in front of you about 10 cm off the floor to take the strain off this part of your body. Your feet should also preferably be resting at an angle rather like on the pedals of a car.

General working conditions

Of course, none of this will do any good if you forget about your posture and start hunching over your screen and keyboard like the Phantom of the Opera anyhow. Remember to check from time to time that your back and neck are straight and your shoulders are pushed back.

Buying an ergonomic chair, keyboard and screen is perhaps the most important investment you can make. If you intend to be working for several hours a day, then it is essential that such a large part of your life is not spent in an uncomfortable position that is bad for your health.

As mentioned in a previous section, it may be a good idea to separate your home life from your working life by setting up an office in a separate room of your home or even renting an office or coworking space, too. For some people, it is psychologically more productive to physically separate work from home life in this way, and you may even make some useful business contacts by sharing office space. I also know of good translator colleagues in different countries who are in contact via Skype with their speakers switched on as if they were sitting together in the same office, keeping each other company while they work!

In the end, all of these suggestions depend on the individual. Only you know how and when you work and concentrate best.

Office exercises

There are plenty of useful exercises to be found on the internet or in person (e.g. yoga or Pilates) to avoid the typical kinds of physical problems brought on by a desk-bound job, but the most important thing they all have in common is stretching.

Here are some simple exercises you can follow whilst working to make sure you stay flexible. All of them should be done slowly, inhaling when making a physical exertion, then exhaling when relaxing. (Incidentally, for useful breathing to calm you down, inhale slowly through your nose and use your diaphragm, not your chest (place one hand on your belly, another on your chest to check) so that you're using the "bottom" of your lungs, not just the top as in shallow breathing when we're tense or angry.)

If you think you may have a fairly serious muscle problem or something similar, then you should really consult a doctor before doing even these simple exercises, but in general you should be able to do these from time to time while you work.

-    Stand up and sit down repeatedly a few times once in a while. Yes, that simple.

-    Shrug your shoulders, as if you've just rejected a pathetic fee. Move them up, back, down then forward in a circular motion at the same time, then just one, then the other.

-    Nod and shake your head very slowly several times and move it in slow circles to keep your neck muscles in motion.

-    Stretch one arm out in front of you with the fingers stretching upwards as if pushing an object away from you, then pull those fingers back towards you slowly with your other hand to stretch them some more. Repeat with the other hand. Then do the opposite with the fingers pointing downwards, pulling your fingers in towards you.

-       With one arm outstretched, grab the elbow or upper arm with the other hand from below and pull it across your chest, all the while still facing forward without twisting your torso. Hold it for a few seconds, then release. Then the other arm.

-       Hug yourself. Seriously. Grab your shoulders and see how hard and tightly you can hug yourself, holding the position while breathing slowly in and out. Then stretch your arms out wide and back, making circles with your hands.

-       Do a facepalm, as if your client has forgotten to send you the text. Push your palm against your forehead and push your head against it, maintaining the pressure for a few seconds. Do the same on the sides and back of your head. Also try tilting your head sideways, and moving your ear towards your shoulder, whilst looking forward at the screen without twisting. If this is difficult, try placing your hand on the opposite side of your head (e.g. left hand on right side of head) and pulling against your head as your head resists.

-       Sit upright and stretch your hands high above your head, intertwining your fingers. Look up at the ceiling and flex your outstretched hands so that the palms face upwards, then downwards.

-       Sit forward, pushing your chair away from the desk, and place your hands and arms beneath your thighs. Let your head hang loose and relaxed. Now try to hug your legs towards you as tightly as possible.

-       Grabbing the armrests (or the bottom of your chair if it has none), see how far you can twist your torso around while keeping your head upright and straight, trying to look behind yourself.

- Pushing your chair away from the desk a little, raise your feet off their rest and hold them outstretched in front of you for ten seconds. "Point" your toes as far away from yourself as much as possible, then try "pointing" them upwards and if possible slightly towards yourself. Move them to the left and right.

As mentioned above, it is usually more efficient, both mentally and physically, to work on a text in bursts of about twenty-five minutes with five-minute breaks than to work for three gruelling hours on end with a half-hour break. You can use these short breaks to get up, stretch and walk around a bit, forgetting all about the translation or your computer for a few minutes. Try not to use the break to check out Facebook, even on your phone; give your eyesight, body and mind a proper rest.[13]

Far better than all of this, of course, is to get regular exercise. In translation, you'll find that you either have too much work or too little, but it is essential to make sure you get some sort of exercise for at least half an hour a day, if possible with a trainer or regular class to push you that little bit further and increase your level of fitness. It also helps to release psychological tension and stress, improving your mental efficiency in general.

Healthy body, healthy mind.

---

[13] If you really want to disconnect completely in your breaks, check out *The One Moment Master* by Martin Boroson.

Specialising: Scientific and Technical Texts for Beginners

One of the many misconceptions held by monolingual people (and potential clients) with little idea about our work is that we know lots of languages. When you tell them you are a translator, they often ask: "How many languages do you speak?" There are in fact two misconceptions implied in this question: firstly, that translators speak, not write (confusing us with interpreters), and secondly that we necessarily speak several languages. In fact, it is not the number of languages that makes a good translator, but their in-depth, specialised knowledge of them.

As a colleague once famously said: "I translate science". This is also my case within certain fields, as well as other specialised areas. Having begun my translation work through engineering (twenty-five ago in a research centre), I have often faced suspicion from linguists who wonder what on earth I'm doing "invading their territory". However, when faced with translations of scientific papers or mechanical patents, these people grudgingly accept that I may be able to translate texts they themselves won't touch. That said, this suspicion is mutual; I have also faced it from engineers who wonder why they need a translator ("What do linguists know about bridge construction?"). These attitudes give rise to more misconceptions such as the myth that "good grammar doesn't matter in technical texts". It is a sobering thought that a misplaced comma in the emergency procedures for a nuclear power station or an aircraft maintenance manual could have catastrophic results. Imagine we see the request:

"Press button?"

There is then a huge difference between:

"No, danger."

or

"No danger."

But who is "qualified" to translate such texts? A monolingual scientist? A scientifically illiterate linguist? There is perhaps a need to reverse the negative attitude of certain linguists towards scientists "invading their turf" and to encourage them to do likewise – "invade" the area of science, where there is good money to be made and you are needed, whatever some engineers may tell you.

Of course, the social divide between the world of science and the world of literature is nothing new. Chemical Engineering students rarely hang out at the weekend with students of Renaissance Literature or Journalism. This continues into their professional careers until their paths inevitably meet, for example when a biochemist needs their research paper translated or edited for publication in an international journal.

Fortunately, the key to writing scientific and technical texts well and clearly is simple: write well and clearly. Period. Take two of the most universal luminaries from the worlds of literature and science: Shakespeare and Einstein. They are both renowned for some of their most famous expressions, such as "To be or not to be" or "$E=mc^2$". Both statements are simple and pithy, yet contain an incredible amount of universal implications. But to come up with such results of genius, much work was necessary beforehand. Such simple, clear text that the layperson can understand is only deceptively simple. Thought and preparation is needed to create it.

Before we look at how to do so, let me stress that people who have learned to master different languages are by definition intelligent people, and therefore perfectly capable of learning new subjects, especially if they decide to specialise. And the wide

146

world of science has enormous possibilities for specialising in something you like (astronomy, the environment, marine biology, medicine, sustainable architecture, antique motorcycle maintenance, etc.). The problem is that many who have only studied linguistics believe that this is an esoteric world of microbiology druids whose secretive terminology is accessible only to a chosen few. This is a strange attitude in people who boast of having a greater vocabulary than most.

As I mentioned in a previous section, it is possible to find a simple definition of the word *isomer* in the Wikipedia or even in a simple, medium-sized monolingual dictionary. You should therefore not be put off by such relatively simple vocabulary—after all, you are a translator and should find no surprises in such a dictionary. (Take note, by the way—for scientific translation you will also need a monolingual dictionary. There is little point knowing that *isomer* in Spanish is *isómero* if you still have no idea what the word means in your own language.) My point is, science is not so mysterious nor the texts so difficult as you may think at first. In fact, you'll probably find that the average 15-year-old high school student is familiar with isomers, as you yourself probably were at that age before your linguistic specialisation led you to forget half the things you learned at school. This is a common drawback in education in the developed world. Again, it works both ways – I once had an engineering client who didn't know what an adjective is. This may explain why many believe that there are no Da Vincis or Aristotles around today, which is quite untrue—they just specialise now. I myself know a production engineer for a multinational glass manufacturer who studied Fine Arts, and a globetrotting trouble-shooter for the cement industry with a degree in Philosophy. As translators, we are condemned to be cultivated and always win at Trivial Pursuit—but there's a green wedge to be won too if you wish to show just how cultivated you truly are. Science is also culture, and it changes the world and society far more than any poet, politician or preacher. And it therefore provides a seemingly infinite amount of texts to be translated.

Even your knowledge of cultural differences can be very useful when translating scientific and technical texts, as we shall see in various ways. There is the infamous example of the Mars Climate Orbiter, which disintegrated on entry into the planet's atmosphere due to a discrepancy in the units of measurement used (the international system of units (metric) and US customary units). A translator proofreading their texts might well have spotted the error.

There are basically two distinct kinds of text: scientific and technical. The former are usually of a standard layout—Abstract, Method, Results, Conclusions/Discussion and Bibliography/References, rounded off by effusive Acknowledgements for the translator, preferably with your email address. These are often written by academics with fairly good linguistic competence and a sound knowledge of the relevant vocabulary, to be published in international journals intended for scientifically literate readers. Technical translations, on the other hand, can provide more problems and should be taken with some humour if you are not to end up banging your head against your keyboard and sobbing loudly. They are often written by private company technicians with scant regard for such trifles as commas and full stops/periods, and are also intended for the layperson who may not have an impressive level of literacy or educational background.

A classic example is provided by instructions manuals. One may well be mistaken for thinking that everybody reads instructions manuals in the same way. This is not entirely true; even cultural issues come into play again.

Consider monochronic and polychronic cultures. In monochronic ("single time") countries and cultures, people generally like to do one thing at a time. They queue in a long line, one behind the other. They are punctual and like to stick to pre-arranged plans, step-by-step. Multi-tasking is not for them. Polychronic people, on the other hand, don't mind too much if you are late. They chop and change plans with relative ease.

As a person brought up in a monochronic culture who now lives in a polychronic one, the culture shock I myself found on arrival was significant. I would walk into a shop to see a mass of people milling about in "the queue" and wonder what to do. Friends would turn up for dinner two hours late. And translation clients would change the project half-way through.

To see how this can affect our texts, let us first take the example of the mobile/cell phone manual, a technical text which we are probably all familiar with and which some of you may even have actually bothered to read. In polychronic cultures, the procedure after purchasing a mobile/cell phone is as follows:

1. Open box.

2. Throw away pesky bits of paper (i.e. instructions manual and guarantee).

3. Proceed to fiddle with buttons and moveable parts for 5 days until:

    a) You realize you don't know how the phone works.

    b) You receive an electric shock.

    c) The phone breaks.

4. Look for instructions manual (being chewed by cat/dog and/or at bottom of bin).

5. Discover phone is indeed broken and/or parts are missing and/or it is in fact an electric razor.

6. Look for guarantee.

7. Discover 5-day trial period has now expired.

8. Curse manufacturer.

In monochronic cultures, however, the procedure can be quite different:

1. Open box.

2. Proceed to read instructions manual step-by-step for 5 days.

3. Take phone out of cellophane. (Place cellophane out of reach of children as instructed.)

4. See points 5 to 8 above.

The point is, instructions are read differently depending on who reads them, and this should in theory affect how they should be written. In polychronic climes, people often skip "boring bits" and prefer to discover the product for themselves, using the instructions only as a reference when they come across something they don't understand. This implies avoiding the use of pronouns or references to other sections, even if you end up being repetitive. Technical texts are not meant to be works of art, but to be unequivocal and unambiguous. Indeed, *many of the rules that should be applied to instructions manuals can be applied to legal texts, too.*

Apart from cultural preferences, there may also be other reasons for skipping points. Take emergency procedures. All companies have two possible emergency procedures in the event of a fire, for example. Let us call them plan 'a' and plan 'b'. Plan 'a' involves following a well-rehearsed drill and assembling staff at a pre-arranged meeting point. Plan 'b' involves racing round like headless chickens, arms flailing, screaming for dear life. Unfortunately, when people's lives are in imminent danger, it is plan 'b' that prevails.

So let us imagine a fire breaks out in a factory. Our hapless hero worker seizes an extinguisher and begins to read the instructions with understandably great haste:

1- Congratulations on purchasing your X-300 fire extinguisher, the top of the range bla bla bla.

A ball of flame flares up, searing the seat of their pants.

2- Ensure this apparatus is cleaned every two months according to European guideline 1:200-F. Begin by carefully applying a damp cloth, etc.

As the hair on the back of their neck begins to singe, they will obviously quickly skip the next few seemingly irrelevant points, jumping to point 10:

10- Connect the former to the latter and turn in the same direction as in point 5.

At this point the worker wisely decides to wield the extinguisher as a hefty weapon with life-or-death ferocity, mercilessly beating a ruthless warpath through the pack of panic-stricken people blocking the emergency exit (indicated in Diagram 'h' of Emergency Procedure Appendix II). At least it came in handy.

Clearly, essential points should be brief and come first, points 1 and 2 (above) should come later if at all in publicly visible emergency instructions, and full nouns should be used rather than "former" and "latter". Again, one should avoid references to other points that may have been omitted by the reader.

Such rules when writing technical texts and instructions can be found in "controlled languages" created artificially for this very purpose. These are used in multinational joint ventures where people from many countries are involved and where English is used as the common language but the employees' grasp of this language is not perfect. One such example is ASD-STE100 (Simplified Technical English). Such rules, while helping to prevent misunderstandings, inevitably lead to a repetitive style, which in turn leads to a high degree of translation memory fuzzy matches. This fact has not been lost on some companies that have even produced controlled languages with this in mind (e.g. Caterpillar and CLOUT).

As these artificial grammars are extremely expensive to buy and very long, I have condensed what we might call "technical grammar" into 10 golden rules to keep in mind when writing instructions manuals (and legal contracts).

10 rules for simplified language

1. Don't use the passive (or reflexives etc. in other languages).

E.g.:
The knob is turned clockwise. ×
Turn the knob clockwise. ✓

Although both phrases are grammatically correct, we should avoid the use of the passive voice in English. This is because people with a low literacy level or users of English as a second language may be more easily confused when changing the word order of the subject and object. (*Note: According to the UK's National Literacy Trust, the average reading age among adults is that of a 13-year-old.[14] About 7 million adults in the UK[15] and 70 million in the US[16] read and write well below the functional literacy level (at which such skills are useful to us in our daily life).*)

Try to use the imperative instead. People are also more likely to follow "commands" in polychronic cultures rather than "polite suggestions". It is better to *tell* such people not to walk on the grass than to advise them that the authorities would appreciate it greatly.

----

[14] Oxford Guide to Plain English.

[15] UK Government, "Skills for Life".

[16] *Illiteracy Statistics. A Numbers Game.* New York Times.

2. Use short sentences.

In English, sentences should generally be of fewer than 20 words for instructions manuals.

Once, when driving to talk at a congress at a university I hadn't been to before, I used my car's satnav GPS device to choose my route. I should have done so before setting out on my journey, of course, but as I was in a hurry I rather foolishly did so on a quiet, straight stretch of road. However, during the process I was asked on the screen about possible toll roads ahead:

"Some of the roads ahead before reaching your destination are toll roads, so could you indicate if you would like to avoid toll roads? YES/NO."

This is rather a long sentence to digest while driving. Not wanting to take my eyes off the road, I read *toll roads* and *YES/NO*, believing that I was being asked whether or not I wanted to travel on toll roads. In fact, the screen was asking if I wanted to *avoid* them. So I ended up choosing the wrong option. This is a classic case of a long sentence confusing the rushed reader. (Even if I had not been driving, there may have been another cause of hurry or distraction.) It is also obvious that the device is referring to roads between my current location and my destination, so much of the information in the sentence is superfluous.

It would have been more sensible to simply write:

"Do you want toll roads? YES/NO."

3. One idea per sentence.

Bullet points and numbers can be used, as we are doing in these ten rules. As a translator and writer, you are undoubtedly capable of using many literary grammatical resources to write varied, interesting sentences with different structures for different effects on the target readers. However, the only purpose in technical writing is to ensure that there is no ambiguity. The text must be as simple as possible with no possibility of misunderstanding by the reader. Again, we could say the same of legal texts. Indeed, all of these rules should ideally also be applied to such texts, though unfortunately lawyers themselves often seem to believe otherwise...advise them!

4. A logical, chronological order of activity.

As in point 3, we should avoid writing flowery, advanced text with a sophisticated word order, as this may lead to confusion by foreign or hurried readers, or else readers with a low level of literacy. To sum up points 2, 3 and 4, let's look at an example.

E.g.:

Before switching on the machine, you should always check that there is nothing obstructing the paper exit and ensure that the protective covering has been removed.

×

Notice that, in the "incorrect" example above, the idea of switching on the machine appears first in the sentence. Somebody working hurriedly, distractedly or with an inadequate grasp of English may simply switch on the machine immediately after reading these words before continuing to read the sentence, as in a step-by-step, monochronic approach. To avoid this potential danger, in the "correct" example we should put the instructions in the same chronological order in which they are to be carried out.

The "incorrect" example above is also long (>20 words) and includes various ideas in the same sentence, whereas it would be clearer to separate each idea into complete, short phrases.

A better way of phrasing the example, then, would be:

- *Check:*

i. *Nothing is obstructing the paper exit.*
ii. *You have removed the protective covering.*

- *Now switch on the machine.*

✓

5. Avoid synonyms.

E.g.:

Take machine *out* of box, *remove* protective wrapping and *take off* plastic tabs.

×

- *Remove* the machine from the box.

- *Remove* the protective wrapping.

- *Remove* the plastic tabs.

✓

Here, the problem with the "incorrect" sentence is that the reader may possibly think that the words *take out*, *remove* and *take off* are actually three very different instructions. Phrasal verbs can also be somewhat confusing for users of English as a second language.

By using the word *remove* repeatedly, the reader has no doubt that it means the same thing. If they need to check the meaning in a dictionary, they only have to look once.

This principle is also very important in advanced scientific texts, where fairly simple everyday words may also have another very specific significance in a particular field (such as "Christmas trees" for oil drilling). By using synonyms in a translation, you may inadvertently be using some specific, advanced terminology and changing the meaning of the text entirely.

6. Always use articles and demonstratives.

E.g.:

Take machine out of box, remove protective wrapping and take off plastic tabs.

×

- *Remove **the** machine from **the** box.*

- *Remove **the** protective wrapping.*

- *Remove **the** plastic tabs.*

✓

The purpose of this is particularly for clarity as regards non-native readers. **The** use of **the** article makes **the** nouns easily identifiable. (In English, many nouns can be used as verbs with no change, for example.) It also specifies that we are talking about the same *tabs* just mentioned, for example, just in case there are others in the machine or factory etc. that the reader may mistakenly understand to be mentioned here if they have skipped points.

7. Avoid pronouns.

E.g.:

*- Insert the **former** into the **latter** and press **it**.*

×

*- Insert **the plug** into **the socket** and press **the button***

✓

Again, the problem here arises if the polychronic or rushed reader skips sections. To avoid confusion, we need to repeat the nouns. This leads to a very repetitive, boring style. Nonetheless, technical texts are not meant to be works of literary art, but to be unequivocally clear. Once again, the same applies to legal texts (in theory!).

8. Avoid references to other sections.

E.g.:

- *"Repeat the action in Rule 7."*

×

- *"Insert the plug into the socket and press the button."*

✓

As with the use of pronouns, the problem here arises if the polychronic or rushed reader skips sections. To avoid confusion, we need to repeat entire sections. This leads to a very repetitive, boring style. Nonetheless, technical texts are not meant to be works of literary art, but to be unequivocally clear. Once again, the same applies to legal texts (in theory!).

You have probably noticed that I have just used practically the same paragraph as in the previous point 7, precisely for the same reason! A nice fuzzy match. ☺

Where reasonably possible, we should also avoid references to other sections in the manual or contract, writing the entire section out again in full if necessary and practical (unless the section is very large, for example).

9. Use "simple" words found in general dictionaries.

E.g.:

Employ straightforward words and utilize uncomplicated expressions. Eschew convoluted phrases.

×

Use simple words and expressions. Avoid complex phrases.

✓

Clearly, when writing a technical text for the layperson who may not have a high educational level, we need to keep the vocabulary simple. As mentioned above, however, we need to take care to ensure that apparently simple words do not actually have a very specific meaning in a specific field, though much more so in advanced scientific texts than in simple instructions manuals.

10. Use complete sentences.

E.g.:

- Continue?

×

- Do you want to continue?

✓

Here, we need to beware that the grammar and therefore meaning of the sentence may be misunderstood. For example, in the "bad" example, the reader may think they are simply being asked to check if the machine is continuing to work, as opposed to being asked if they want to stop it.

10. Check the numbering.

If you're good at proofreading, you will hopefully have noticed that this is in fact the eleventh point, not the tenth. As in legal texts such as contracts, the authors may add sections, clauses or appendices at the last moment, changing the numbering and order of the subsequent sections. They may well forget to check that cross-references made to different sections are now wrong.

If the manual or contract says "*See section 7*", make sure it really is referring to that section.

You may be able to improve your client's source text with such tips as these. As pointed out above, this kind of plain English is also useful in legal texts, not to mention any text aimed at the general public whose literacy levels may not be the same as ours.

The European Union also has a guide called "How to write clearly" in various languages that you can download for free:

http://ec.europa.eu/translation/documents/clear_writing_tips_en.pdf

You can use this to back you up if your client doesn't understand why you have shortened or changed their text.

More questions for the client

Should I translate the words printed on the product?

English is rather an internationally accepted language in science and engineering, with the result that words such as *on/off* are practically universal common knowledge. As such, they are often written physically on machines and devices. Therefore, we obviously shouldn't translate them in the text (or at most only put the translation in brackets next to the English words). We need to ask the client in any case to make sure this is the case.

Danger or caution?

Words such as *danger*, *hazard*, *warning*, *caution* and *notice* represent different levels of safety. In precautionary statements, they may in fact represent very specific safety standards and regulations. We therefore need to be careful about translating them arbitrarily. Check with the client if this is pertinent and if possible obtain the specific rules to which such terms apply. If the two countries in question are in the EU, for example, there should be a direct, specific and official translation we must use. You can check out EC/EEC directives in various languages here:

http://eur-lex.europa.eu/.

What regulations does the product comply with?

Talking of regulations, different countries have different rules. While your client's product may comply with the law, regulations and standards in the USA (e.g. ANSI, OSHA), if they are importing it into the EU this may be irrelevant in the text for the target readers. Ask the client if they know what regulations it applies to in the target country. They should know. If not, you will have warned them of a potential problem.

The company may have its own internal regulations with its own codes, too. If so, ask for the key and if they already have a corporate glossary. If it is a multinational, they may even already have a multilingual one.

What are the units of measurement?

As seen in the case of the Mars Climate Orbiter, it is essential to agree on the units to be used in the text, most probably the common units in the target reader's country. Is the client aware of this? Do you have to convert the numbers? (If so, consider charging extra if it's a lot of work, and warn them if you're not too sure about doing it well; we aren't mathematicians.)

Remember that different languages have different numerical notations, too, such as decimal points or commas and different ways of expressing units of thousands. A billion is not the same in different languages and countries, either.

What do these letters mean?

In technical translations, the source text may be poorly written (surprise, surprise...). It is crucial that you check this before accepting the job, as with any kind of text. There may be acronyms and abbreviations used only internally by the corporation that it is impossible to even guess at. Does the client want them translated, too? (If so, you should provide a key to the translated acronyms and abbreviations along with the translated text.)

Does the client know the terminology?

It is quite possible that the authors of a technical text, and particularly of a scientific text, are well aware of the correct target terminology, especially in English. They may sell their product abroad or be very familiar with texts on the same matter in international scientific journals. If this is the case, they may opt to translate the text themselves (!) and want you to "simply" check that their final text is well written in terms of grammar, style and punctuation, etc. Ask them if this is the case or if they expect you to check that all of the terminology is correct, too (which may take much longer). Get this in writing, not only on the phone.

Only you can decide if you truly understand the text. If it is not one of your fields or extremely complicated and you're still not sure after a little research on the internet, then be honest and decline or say that you will only proofread or review their translated text, not confirm the correct terminology.

Useful search ideas

Ask the client first

One of the obstacles to understanding poorly written technical source texts may be the lack of context. You may get a list of computer strings, for example, where the client is unaware that the word order changes on translating the sentences to another language with another syntax, which will now make no sense in the translation. Or maybe they will send you a list of machine parts with no context, using vague, ambiguous words such as *rod, slider* or *belt*. If your crystal ball is not working, you may have to ask the client for clarification to decide on the translation in the precise context. This can come in the form of supporting documents for more context, similar brands' websites (but beware of using the other companies' terminology/trademarks) and pictures.

Pictures

Diagrams and photos are sometimes invaluable for understanding technical texts such as the parts of a boat, bridge or even the human body (e.g. Google Zygote Body). You can use the Google Images search or online picture dictionaries such as the Merriam-Webster online. Then there are industrial sales hubs such as www.DirectIndustry.com where you can find the same products in different languages with photos, described by the companies that produce them.

Wikipedia: good or bad?

Of course, the ultimate picture dictionary is an encyclopaedia, and perhaps the ultimate encyclopaedia today is Saint Wiki. As explained earlier, Wikipedia should not be used as a reference for correct terminology, but as a learning tool it has its uses, especially if you need to understand scientific and technical texts. However, first perhaps it is necessary to explain just how to use it wisely— and how not to.

The Wikipedia is a site that depends entirely on contributions— both in terms of financing and information. The articles are written by volunteers, which should obviously set alarm bells ringing as to its reliability as a dictionary. Sometimes you'll find a symbol next to the language that has been defined as a "good article" (often in German!), and the site applies a "verifiability" policy which means that all pages should cite sources whose reliability you can then check. So why use it at all? Well, its reliability is proportional to the simplicity of the subject matter, due to its democratic form of editing. For example, if you decide to write an article about kangaroos, saying that they are a kind of gigantic mollusc that lives in the Arctic Ocean, it will immediately be removed by Wikepedians with more authoritative knowledge than yours on the world's fauna, not least because they have a "no original research" policy and the idea of huge polar molluscs is, well, quite original. If, however, you decide to give the world the benefit of your meagre knowledge about erythropoiesis in haemopoietic tissue, there will be far fewer people qualified to dispute you if you affirm that it is caused, say, by ingesting huge Arctic gastropods (though you'll have to provide prior research into the phenomenon, which could be tricky). In other words, the Wikipedia is the Sesame Street of science. It's where Grover explains isomers to you, and in this respect it does indeed work and can be an invaluable self-learning tool.

171

Another important point to note about Wikipedia is that the texts in different languages are often written by different authors and so may bear absolutely no relation to each other. In other words, the texts are different and this may even lead to slightly differing definitions.

After learning about the text's subject matter via Wikipedia, we should then use more reliable sources for the translation itself (there may be some useful citations on the same Wikipedia page).

Corpora

Corpora are large groups of texts often used for statistical linguistic studies but which can also be used to see if an expression is commonly used in a certain country or field. One famous example is Springer Link (link.springer.com). This has many specific scientific fields and gives search results according to content type, discipline, publication and language. You can also find the period in which the texts were published, if this is relevant (e.g. If your text is from the 1970s and talks about *spam*, it will be referring to processed meat, not junk emails). A simple concordance/collocation tool is also provided by Google itself with its Ngram viewer. (When writing this book, I used this to check if people usually write *e-mail* or *email*, *Internet* or *internet*. The former are still more popular in print at the time of writing, apparently, but this seems to be changing, so I opted for the latter!) Sketch Engine is a useful, user-friendly corpus, too. As for honing down your specific searches further, you could do worse than investing in Intelliwebsearch.

As modern translators, we should master Google searches anyhow to save our own time and ensure accuracy. This involves using quotation marks to find words in the same order, asterisks to indicate missing words, etc. I am not going to bore you or pad this book out with the details here, since you can easily find all such information well explained by Google itself and even ask questions

(e.g.: http://www.google.com/insidesearch/tipstricks/all.html).

I will mention, however, the type of document search, as this may be handy in finding that elusive Word document. In the Google search box, simply type _filetype:_ followed immediately by the type of file you wish to find (_pdf, ppt_ (PowerPoint), _doc_ (Word), _xls_ (Excel) etc.). The type of site search can also hone down your search to relevant, reliable sources (_site:_ followed by the kind of sites among which you wish to search, such as _edu_ (educational), _org_ (often used by schools, non-profit organisations, etc.)).

Then there is Google Scholar, the search engine's academic version. You can use it to find texts published by research centres and universities, for example.

Nevertheless, when it comes to scientific translation, in my experience the clients are usually very understanding anyhow, well aware that their specialised jargon is unfathomable to most of the population. If they have time, they are sometimes willing to explain complex concepts to you, especially if they are from the academic world. Indeed, they may even be pleased that you are taking such an interest and ensuring you have fully understood their text.

Scientific Texts

By *Scientific Texts*, I am referring mainly to reports on studies and experiments to be published in scientific journals, for example.

They generally follow a standard layout something like this:

- Abstract

- Method

- Results

- Conclusions (often called "Discussion", particularly if the conclusions are unsatisfactory!)

- Acknowledgements

- Bibliography/References

Abstract

This is where your skills as a writer are truly needed. It is a very short section following the title and authors, maybe of just a hundred words, summarising the entire experiment, clinical trial or whatever. You may even suggest to your client that you could write this yourself according to their needs instead of translating their text, since you may even do a better job. It is basically the text that is used to "sell" the paper to an international journal, for example. Technically, as it is simply a summary of what is to follow, it more or less follows the same order as the entire text.

An interesting method used for writing abstracts is known as the CARS model (Create A Research Space). It is basically a step-by-step way of creating a marketing text for scientists (i.e. the abstract), like this:

First, we **establish a research area**. This means giving the background (other previous research, the scientific field, etc.), preferably suggesting that our client is an expert and that this paper is essential in the matter.

Next, we **establish a niche within this research area** (thus indicating why this particular paper is so important and interesting). This may involve disputing a previous claim, filling a gap in human knowledge, posing a question or advancing current research lines.

Finally, we **occupy this niche**, thereby indicating that this paper is about solving a problem. To do so, we state the general purposes of the paper or describe current research (for example, in studies of scientific literature to get an idea of the current general situation). Then we state the findings the authors have made and give a rough idea of the layout of the paper that follows.

Another easier way to remember this and the paper's layout vaguely, in my opinion, is by looking at the story of Odysseus. All Hollywood action movies follow the same general script as the Greek hero. First, there is an injustice or terrible occurrence (here, a gap in knowledge or a mistaken belief, for example). Then our hero has to go through lots of adventures (the method) which have specific consequences in the end (the results). Finally, our hero metes out justice and we learn or discuss the moral of the story (the conclusion/discussion). Then at the very end, up go the credits (acknowledgements and references).

Perhaps it is no surprise that the ancient Greeks had such an influence on science and the way we write it! We shall look more deeply at their influence in other aspects of scientific writing later.

Method

This section explains how the experiment, research, trial, survey, etc. was carried out. It gives details of apparatus, substances, software, parameters, amounts, samples, study subjects, etc. and possibly previous examples of research with their similarities or differences, explaining these.

It is often called "Methodology" these days, though technically this would mean the "study of methods"! (I often attempt to point this out to the authors, to little avail as they seem to think I am being a pedantic grammar Nazi—but, hey, that's my job.)

Results

Like the Method, this section is usually quite detailed and technical. *You should take a look at these two sections (Method and Results) to see if you are going to be able to confidently understand and translate the text.* The Results section may also include some mathematics, perhaps the most difficult of all fields to translate.

Here, the authors describe the findings, perhaps describing statistical methods and software used, margins of error, etc., often with graphs and tables. (Check you can change the text in these, as well as if any text in them appears in the word count.)

Conclusions/Discussion

This is self-explanatory. Here, the authors explain what the results actually mean. They attempt to show the importance of their findings and the new knowledge gleaned that the scientific world should know about.

Acknowledgements

Try to get acknowledgement for the translator; you deserve it.

Bibliography / References

Ask the authors if they want this translated, proofread or left untouched. (If it's not too long, proofread it anyway. I usually find spelling mistakes and the client is pleased to be notified of them. Remember to check the spelling of authors' names on the internet.)

The client may even leave this section out altogether when sending you the text if they don't want it translated. If this is the case, ask them for it anyhow, because this section is actually rather important for the translator. The reason for this is that this section contains much of the terminology that the authors have used in writing the text, usually with many of the translations in texts of different languages. In fact, *I would advise looking at this section before you start translating the text* in order to gather the relevant vocabulary.

Don't spend ages doing terminology searches only to discover the lexis is right here at the end of the same text!

Search Tips for Science

Chemical notation

If we want to know the name of a chemical compound in another language, one way is to find its chemical notation first. For example, ethanol or ethyl alcohol (the kind we find in beer and wine) can be written with this notation: C_2H_6O. By looking up this notation in other languages, we can find its name. However, we need to be aware of isomers, since there may be more than one form:

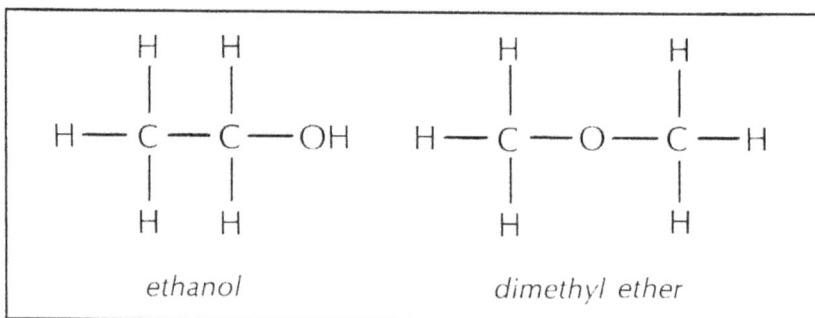

ethanol   dimethyl ether

(Alcohols can also be written with OH at the end to distinguish them, as in C_2H_5OH.)

Chemical notation can change slightly from Asian to European languages, too. You can also look up the World Health Organisation's list of proposed International Non-Proprietary Names (INN) for chemicals: http://ec.europa.eu/health/documents/community-register/html/inn_full.htm.

These give the scientific name as opposed to brand names or other approved names (e.g. British Approved Name (BAN) or

United States Approved Name (USAN)). For example, acetylsalicylic acid is more commonly known as *aspirin*. Hence, you can find their corresponding official scientific translations (and possibly avoid using brand names from companies that have patented a chemical product (similar considerations may be applied to technical translations)).

Note that pharmaceutical names in languages other than English often take an article (e.g. *La aspirina* in Spanish).

Latin and Greek roots

One useful trick to help check the names of flora and fauna is to look for the Latin name that scientists have generally agreed upon to find the corresponding common name in each respective language. For example, if we know that a holm oak is *Quercus ilex*, it is then relatively easy to find the more common name in other languages from reputable sources. This is important because there is quite a lot of unreliable information in websites that can confuse the more common names, as well as the possibility of regional variations in common names within the same country.

Evidently, if we thoroughly understand the underlying concepts behind the Greek and Latin terminology, there is far less possibility of making mistakes as we will have a feel for the right language. Fortunately, this does not mean we have to learn Greek or Latin! By having a basic understanding of the building blocks of the vocabulary—the Latin and Greek roots (suffixes and prefixes)—we need not remember huge amounts of botanical, zoological or medical terms, for example.

Many of the Latin roots used in scientific vocabulary originally came from Greek long ago. "New" Latin largely absorbed this lexis and adapted it, particularly during the era when cultivated

Romans and learned Greeks were very much bilingual. "Old" Latin vocabulary was used mainly for business, administrative, and legal purposes (where it can still be found today), whereas the immigrant Greek eggheads used their native tongue for philosophical and scientific pursuits, and from there this vocabulary was passed on to "New" Latin. Much of this Greek and, later, Latin knowledge was translated into Arabic with the rise of the Moors in medieval times, who in turn added their new scientific findings to the literature. These writings were then translated back to Latin from Arabic by Christian monks such as the great boffin Constantine the African, contributing significantly to the widespread use of Latin in science. Ironically, then, the West learned of the works of Hippocrates and Galen of Pergamon through translations from Arabic. Medical and scientific knowledge was later finally translated into the vernacular. Fortunately for most English-speaking translators, however, English is now the modern-day Latin in terms of cross-cultural medical and scientific language.

So let's look at how those building blocks of much scientific and medical language—the Latin (and Greek) roots—work.

Binomials

Before we look at a simple way to understand the Latin terminology itself, it may be useful to briefly see word the order in which the Latin descriptions of living organisms are written to describe flora and fauna:

(Life > Domain >) Kingdom > Phylum > Class > Order > Family > Genus >Species

Holm oak, for example, would be:

Plantae>Angiosperms>Eudicots>Rosids>

*Fagales>Fagaceae>**Quercus>ilex***

Don't panic! Only the last two words are usually used to identify the life form, since in the text you're translating you will already know if you're talking about trees or herbs from the context. This common, two-word method of naming life forms is known as *binomial* or *binominal* nomenclature, made up of the genus and the species[17].

(Note: the binomial should be written in *italics* and the first word (the genus) should begin with a capital letter (e.g. "holm oak (*Quercus ilex*)"). The genus can be used on its own, whilst the species should always be named alongside its genus, even if the latter is only represented with an initial (e.g. *Quercus i.*). These rules also apply to fungi and bacteria, but not necessarily to viruses, since these were named more recently and so their species names do not necessarily come from Latin. The terms must also agree in terms of Latin grammar, not English or other languages.)

---

[17] For more detail on the nomenclature of life forms, look up Linnaean and evolutionary taxonomy.

The term *angiosperm* to refer to the holm oak tree is another classic example of how we can use Latin roots to truly understand the underlying scientific concepts. *Angio* comes from the Latin for *vessel*. *Sperm* means *seed*. So we have *"seed vessel" (angiosperm)*. The other major kind of seed-bearing tree is known as a *gymnosperm*. *Gymno* means *naked* (the word *gymnastics* came about because the ancient Greeks used to do such sports without wearing a stitch). So we have *"naked seed" (gymnosperm)*.

What then, are *"seed vessels"* and *"naked seeds"*? Well, the former are flowering plants (the flower being the vessel that contains the seed), whereas the latter refers to plants such as conifers that give such joy to hay-fever sufferers as they disperse their naked seeds.

The root *angio*, or *vessel*, is very common in another field of science: medicine. It is used to refer to blood vessels.

In the next section, we'll look at some such roots to begin to decipher apparently complex medical terminology. You'll find it's not so mysterious.

Tips for Medical Translation

Medical translation is perhaps one of those areas where the stakes are the highest if the translator makes a mistake. Considering the specialised knowledge and jargon often required, the prospect of working with these types of texts can seem daunting to those with little experience in the medical field. Nevertheless, medical lexis sometimes appears in texts generally unrelated to medicine, so a basic knowledge of such a universal subject can always come in handy. Furthermore, not every medical text need inspire awe in translators. Nor should we forget that, unfortunately, there will always be a need for medical terminology. So, let's take a look at the possibilities.

Firstly, "medical texts" include a wide range of registers, target readers, and levels of knowledge that may make some of them more accessible to the budding medical translator. They range from in-depth research on new vaccines to leaflets giving public health information. You should be aware that in English-speaking countries the vocabulary can sometimes undergo more changes when shifting register than in countries whose language has Latin roots. This is because, quite simply, a large part of medical terminology is indeed Latin-based. Hippocrates' native tongue is also still used today in this lexis (though often via Latin itself). But while many doctors and researchers may have an excellent grasp of the English language for their specific peer-to-peer communications, they may need to change register to explain concepts to children or the elderly, for example. Or perhaps a pharmaceutical company needs to advertise its new product in another country, taking care to avoid making false claims, touching a cultural nerve, or simply being misunderstood. In some poorer countries with high illiteracy rates, clients may even need to be advised not to translate their material, but instead convey the message using images. Even here, great care is needed. For example, there was the famous case of a powdered milk producer whose logo was a smiling baby. Accustomed to seeing a picture of the product enclosed, the horrified locals believed the company's trucks to be loaded with babies! In other words, good communication with the client and awareness of the target audience is extremely important, as always.

We should not be immediately put off by medical jargon. Again, try to learn about the specific subject you're dealing with for 30 minutes and see if it really is so complicated. The Latin roots we're about to see will help you a great deal in this regard, especially as they are used with only minimal changes in many languages. (Even so, you will need to check your target language against solid resources—or ask your client if they know! You would also do well to search the glossaries to be found on such sites as the US National Institutes of Health and MedilinePlus. If you work with Spanish I heartily recommend Cosnautas.)

As we saw above with Latin binomials to describe life forms, Latin and Greek roots can be used as simple building blocks to describe complex concepts in medicine. If we learn the roots, then we can use them to create much longer terms to define very specific nouns. (This is why science has such a huge vocabulary: genes and inorganic and organic chemistry also have naming systems based on basic building blocks because it is much easier to learn the roots than all of the entire terms themselves, which I daresay would be an impossible task anyhow.)

Many translators know the meaning of *lumbalgia* (more generally known as *lumbago* in English) and *tendinitis* (a.k.a. *tendonitis*). They presumably also know that *lumbar* refers to the lower back and *-itis* usually means an inflammation. So what, then, does the *algia* in *lumbalgia* mean? Not surprisingly, pain (from Greek). Some of you are probably already aware of how Latin and Greek roots can be used to make sense of medical terms. Take the prefix *athr(o)* (of the joints, from Greek), for example, which gives us the word "arthritis" (inflammation of the joints). So, what do you think *athralgia* means? I hope you've worked it out: it is what the layperson refers to as painful joints.

Take a quick look at the examples of Latin and Greek roots listed below and the concepts to which they refer. See how many of them you already recognize.

aden (Gr.): gland

a /an- (Gr.): without

-algia/alge(si)(Gr.): pain

angio (Gr.): [blood] vessel

athro (Gr.): of the joints

brachi(o) (L.): of the arms

brachy (Gr.): short

cardiac/cardial (Gr. & L.): of the heart

-centesis (Gr. & L.): puncturing

-cephaly (Gr. & L.): head

costo (L.) ribs

cyte (from cito (Gr.): cell

-dactyl (Gr. & L.): pertaining to fingers / toes (digits)

dermato (Gr.): of the skin

-ectomy (Gr.): surgical removal

endo (Gr.): inside

erythro (Gr.): red

gastro/gastric (Gr.): of the stomach

gymno (Gr.): naked

hepat- (Gr.): liver

hyper (Gr.): high (too much)

hypo (Gr.): low (too little)

-itis: inflammation (strictly speaking, *-itus* refers to allergies)

leuko/leuco (Gr.): white (pale)

myo (Gr.): muscle

nephro (Gr.): of the kidney

-ology (Gr.): all-encompassing (to refer to the entire specialisation or study)

-oma (Gr.): tumour

oss-, ost-, oste-, osteo (Gr. & L.): of bones

-osis (Gr.): condition, disease or increase

-(o)stomy (Gr.): surgical opening (like a buttonhole) (*NB. stoma (Gr.) – "of the mouth" (in medicine, usually an opening from*

within the body to the outside, naturally or surgically; a figurative "little mouth"))

-(o)tomy (Gr.): surgical incision (in general)

oxy/oxus (Gr.): sharp

pachy (Gr.) : thick

-pathy (Gr.): disease or disorder

-penia/-poenia (Gr.): lowering, deficiency

-plasty (Gr.): involving plastic surgery

-rhino(s): of the nose

-rragia: abnormally large flow

-rrhea (Gr.): discharge, flow

-syn (Gr.): together

thorac(i)-, thorac(o)-, thoracico- (Gr.): chest (also: *steth(o)-* (Gr.))

trachea (Gr.): windpipe (from larynx to bronchi)

In brackets I have shown whether the root originally came from ancient Greek or later Latin. It's not necessary to know this, but it explains the difference in use between the letters "i" and "y" in English, which should not be confused as they may spell different meanings as in *brachi-* and *brachy-*.

Remember that these definitions only apply to medicine; the same vocabulary may mean something else in another field of science. For example, *trachea* is also the tube insects use to convey air, whereas it is a conductive vessel in vascular plants. Even so, you can see that the same original concept (in this case, a tube) can help understand the meaning of the word in different scientific fields.

OK. Now it's your turn! Try to use the roots we've just seen to understand the medical terms on the following pages (I haven't listed all of them, since some should be obvious). See if you can guess what they mean.

Abdominocentesis:

Analgesic:

Angiology:

Angiotomy:

Brachycephaly:

Brachiocephalic:

Endoscope:

Answers on page 194.

Erythrocyte:

Gastrostomy:

Glucopenia:

Hepatology:

Mammaplasty:

Myalgia:

Myectomy:

Answers on page 195.

Nephralgia:

Rhinoplasty:

Nephritis:

Stethalgia:

Syndactyly:

Thyroidectomy:

Answers on page 196

Abdominocentesis: Puncturing of abdomen

Analgesic: Pain killer (= "opposite of pain")

Angiology: The study of the circulatory system (blood vessels)

Angiotomy: Surgical incision into blood vessels

Brachycephaly: Short/flattened head

Brachiocephalic: Referring to head and arms

Endoscope: Instrument for looking inside the body

Back to questions: Page 191.

Erythrocyte: Red blood cell

Gastrostomy: Surgical opening to the stomach.

Glucopenia: Low (blood) sugar count

Hepatology: The study of the liver.

Mammaplasty: Plastic surgery on breasts

Myalgia: Muscular pain

Myectomy: Surgical removal of [part of a] muscle

Back to questions: Page 192.

Nephralgia: Kidney pain

Rhinoplasty: A "nose job" (!)

Nephritis: Inflammation of the kidney.

Stethalgia: Chest pain.

Syndactyly: Fused digits / Digits close together.

Thyroidectomy: Removal of thyroid gland (partial or complete).

Back to questions: page 193.

How did you do? Now try the other way around, "inventing" the more formal medical version of the following concepts, using the Latin and Greek roots provided earlier. Don't worry if you don't get it exactly right. The idea is to see if you are on the right track and have an idea of what expression to expect or look out for. (See next page.)

Headache:

Inflammation of the liver:

Glandular pain:

Severe nosebleed:

Low white blood cell count:

Surgical cutting of rib(s):

High (blood) sugar:

Answers on page 201.

Surgical puncturing of the heart:

Disease of veins or arteries:

Skin inflammation:

Tumours deriving from/around blood vessels:

Liver tumour (usually cancer):

Incision into windpipe:

Answers on page 202.

Of the heart muscle:

Short fingers or toes:

Removal of a gland:

Puncturing the chest to remove fluid:

Artificial opening from large intestine (colon) to outside the body:

Answers on page 203.

Headache: *cephalalgia*

Inflammation of the liver: *hepatitis*

Glandular pain: *adenalgia*

Severe nosebleed: *rhinorrhagia*

Low white blood cell count: *leucopoenia / leukocytopenia*

Surgical cutting of rib(s): *costotomy*

High (blood) sugar: *hyperglycaemia*

Back to questions on page 198.

Surgical puncturing of the heart: *cardiocentesis*

Disease of veins or arteries: *angiopathy*

Skin inflammation: *dermatitis*

Tumours deriving from/around blood vessels: *angioma*

Liver tumour (usually cancer): *hepatoma*

Incision into windpipe: *tracheotomy*

Back to questions on page 199.

Of the heart muscle: *myocardiac*

Short fingers or toes: *brachydactyly*

Removal of a gland: *adenectomy*

Puncturing the chest to remove fluid: *toracocentesis*

Artificial opening from colon to outside body: *colostomy*

Back to questions on page 200.

By learning the etymology of this kind of medical terminology (widely available on the internet), the translator has the great advantage that it is fairly universal and used in many other languages, particularly Romance languages. It is also useful to take into account the singular and plural forms, though don't be surprised if English-speaking doctors simply add their beloved "s" on the end of a word to form plurals, a practice that is now widely considered acceptable or even standard grammar in many cases.

Be aware of your English target audience, too. We Brits and others can be very fond of retaining the "ae" found in Greek roots (*haemo*: of blood), whereas Americans prefer the more phonetically logical "e" (*hemo*). Remember also: oea (U.K.) → ea (U.S.). Very broadly speaking, some common plural endings for medical expressions follow these patterns.

For example:

- -us   →   -i   (e.g., *bronchus* → *bronchi*) (L.)

- -is   →   -es   (e.g., *diagnosis* → *diagnoses*) (L.)

- -um →   -a   (e.g., *ovum* → *ova*) (L.)

- -ex →   -ices   (e.g., *cortex* → *cortices*) (L.)

- -a   →   -ae   (e.g., *bursa* → *bursae*) (L.)

- -a   →   -ata   (e.g., *stoma* → *stomata*) (Gr.)

Abbreviations in medical shorthand

There is one kind of text for which you should perhaps multiply your fees exponentially—doctors' shorthand written notes, such as prescriptions. It remains a mystery to all humanity why physicians in all cultures and languages have handwriting that looks as if a drunken spider has fallen into an inkpot and crawled across the paper. To compound this issue, they also use Latin (though they often do so universally in different languages, which is clearly an advantage to the translator). As if this were not enough, they write in shorthand. First, then, you must decipher the actual symbols scrawled across the page into humanly recognisable characters. (If you are stumped, try asking those who are experts—anyone working in a pharmacy/chemist's—to assist in cracking these hieroglyphs.) The next step is to learn what some of these abbreviations mean. Below are a few common examples used in prescriptions, but you can find many more quite easily on the internet.

- **a.c.** – *ante cibum* – before meals

- **q.d.** – *quaque die* – once a day

- **po/pa/pv** – *per orim* (by mouth) / *per rectum* / *per vagina*

- **q.A.M.** – *Quaque die Ante Meridiem* – every day in the

  morning

- **b.i.d/t.i.d/q.i.d** – *bis/ter/quater in die* – two/three/four

  times a day

You may also see something like "1 – 0 – 1" to indicate that the prescribed pill/medicine is to be taken with one dose in the morning or at breakfast, none at midday, and once at dinner or before going to bed.

To indicate that a symptom is present, a physician may use the symbol "+", and "-" if it is not present. To indicate the symptom's degree of severity, a physician may simply add more ("++" = significant; "+++" = severe).

Abbreviations may be used for days, weeks, months and years (e.g. 2 w = 2 weeks (which may also be written 2/52; or 3 m = 3/12) and the equivalents in other languages). Then there are common shorthand abbreviations that doctors may use to describe symptoms, for example. Here are some fairly common ones in English:

- **Adv:** advised

- **BP:** blood pressure

- **CNS:** central nervous system

- **C/O:** complains of

- **CVS:** cardiovascular system

- **GIS:** gastrointestinal system

- **LLQ:** left lower quadrant (On the abdomen, sometimes written LLQ ABD = *left lower quadrant of **abd**omen*. A GP or family doctor will note down the general location of the pain in this way before referring the patient to a hospital for a more thorough examination. It is seen from the patient's point of view.)

- **MH:** medical history

- **NAD:** nothing abnormal detected

- **O/E:** on examination

- **p. reg.:** regular (normal) pulse

- **RUQ:** right upper quadrant

- **RS:** respiratory system

- **T 90 F:** temperature 90 Fahrenheit

- Δ**:** diagnosis (Greek *delta*)

Medical shorthand exercise

So, let's imagine our patient is being examined by a physician. The exchange might go something like this:

Patient: "I ate some really hot peppers about three days ago and it still hurts. I think I taste blood in my mouth. And yesterday my belly hurt a little right here."

Physician: "Have you or your family had any serious stomach problems before?"

Patient: "Not that I know of."

Physician: "Do you feel any nausea?"

Patient: "Erm…Nope."

Physician: "Eaten anything else unusual lately?"

Patient: "Well, I guess I left those prawns out of the freezer a little too long…"

Physician: "Okay, let's take a look at you and check it out."

…

After the examination, the doctor writes (scrawls):

c/o: Ate hot peppers 3 d ago, injured with fork? + po bleeding, not much. No MH reported. Pain in LUQ ABD. Food poisoning?

o/e: p 80 reg.   BP 95/70. PO: superficial lesion, otherwise normal. T 98 F (po). ABD NAD. Δ Cut tongue. Adv po gel 1-1-1.

The physician's conclusion is that any possible food poisoning has now abated (temperature and abdomen now normal), and that the discomfort and bleeding is due to a superficial fork stab and not to the food itself. A mouth gel is prescribed to be applied 3 times a day.

Or in other words:

The patient complains of having eaten hot peppers 3 days ago. He may have injured himself with a fork. Some bleeding in the mouth; not much. No medical history of the problem reported. Pain in left upper quadrant of the abdomen (as seen from patient's point of view). Possible food poisoning?

On examination: pulse 80, regular. Blood pressure 95/70 (= systolic/diastolic pressure, indicating maximum (when the heart beats) to minimum (when the heart relaxes between beats)). *I see a superficial external lesion. Otherwise mouth normal. Temperature 98 F (taken orally). Nothing abnormal detected in the abdomen. Diagnosis: cut tongue. I have advised using a mouth gel three times a day.*

Capitals for diseases?

Why are some illnesses written with capital letters and others not? The reason is often etymological: diseases named after geographical locations or people take the original capital letter (e.g. Alzheimer's after Alois Alzheimer, and Ebola after the Ebola River).

This section is only intended as a starter to spark interest in technical, scientific or medical translations, the latter primarily through etymology. As translators, we should not fear vocabulary that at first sight seems beyond us. The information provided here is far from authoritative or comprehensive, since it covers only a small facet of an enormous subject. Nor is the etymological approach foolproof, as I have mentioned. There may be confusing expressions such as *cerebellum*/*cerebrum*, *brachy*/*brachi(o)*, and *cardiac*/*cardia*. Reliable references should be used, although Wikipedia can prove useful in providing general information as a very rough means of learning, not for reference. In any case, I hope that you now have a better idea of how to go about tackling this particular kind of medical lexis wherever it may appear in your own specialisations.

And I hope you will now feel less intimidated when you visit your doctor, as you will have some inkling as to what he or she is talking about!

Translation Karma

Dealing with internet trolls

Method 1

Ignore them.

Method 2

Just do Method 1. Really.

But since you've paid for this book, I suppose I should give you the long version.

It is impossible to please everybody in the social networks, even if you are the most polite person on Earth. Some people can be offensive, others easily offended. The bigger your presence in the internet, the more negative comments you will be exposed to. Just try to put it into perspective, since the proportion of these should still be minimal. Even the most successful politicians rarely gain over 50% of the vote. If they were to let this fact get them down, they obviously couldn't do their job.

From time to time, then, you're obviously going to disagree with colleagues on some matters. The important thing is to make sure you side with opinions, not people; both on the screen and in your head. Most people are in fact reasonable and may even change their opinion (or you yourself may do so); there is usually no reason to fall out. If you have a genuine gripe, try at least to treat it with humour if you're going to voice it in the social networks (see the "Confessions" at the end of this book for examples!).

Trolls, on the other hand, are people who don't realise that their belligerence and insults do as much damage (or more) to themselves than to their imagined adversaries. In a previous section, I advised never to make enemies. However, this is clearly an impossible task with trolls, since making enemies is precisely their aim. The only remotely effective thing to do is to walk away; avoid contact just as you should do in real life with such people.

Talking of real life, such negative attitudes don't only exist on the internet. We all know someone who seems to relish complaining all the time about everything. Perhaps they complain to capture people's attention at the dinner table or at a business meeting, but it doesn't necessarily help solve their problems. Indeed, it attracts bad vibes towards the one who is always complaining, just as a cheerful attitude attracts good vibes, inevitably. Studies of salespeople have shown, rather unsurprisingly, that the ones who appear to be happier are the ones who sell the most.

There are people who can spend all day competing with others over who works the hardest, but not about their results. I know some translators who gloomily but proudly boast of how many hours they spend in front of the computer instead of learning how to use hotkeys, voice recognition software or simply learning to type faster (there are many good programs online to improve your typing speed in just a few hours).

Trolls will always have an opinion, whether they are experts or not. Indeed, this book itself has been trolled about its graphic design by a troll who seems to be an expert in translation, graphic design, language teaching…i.e. not an expert in any of them! However, it is obviously better to leave such opinions to the experts instead of listening to a troll's attention-seeking opinion. In this case, I have left the book's graphic design to a paid professional and I trust her opinion over that of an attention-seeking troll. I am not going to give her the unnecessary stress of thinking that I value the opinion of an amateur over hers, just as I don't want a non-professional, non-native proofreader judging my work.

Avoid arguing with trolls and certainly avoid befriending negative people who spend all their free time complaining and gossiping about others or belittling them. And as said above, apply the obvious advice of avoiding insults. When we take care of our words, we end up taking care of our thoughts, too, just as simply forcing a smile can actually cheer us up a little.

Psychologists have also shown that those who forgive others for doing wrong are also far more likely to forgive themselves when they do so, too. This may sound a little egotistical, but it certainly helps them sleep better at night and gain fewer enemies. Take up a kind, forgiving attitude towards others and you'll find the karma will reward you with the same treatment back.

Of course, there are trolls who will never apologise for a wrongdoing, even when they are completely mistaken, those who will never forgive us for our inevitable mistakes (nobody's perfect), and those who think that apologies simply justify meanness. As I pointed out before, in these hopeless cases just limit yourself to the facts. Let them know what has happened, nothing more. At most, possibly let the wrongdoers know that forgiving them for their behaviour does not necessarily mean forgetting. Hopefully they will thus learn that their attitude and actions have real consequences: you have taken note.

These situations may even be beneficial to you, showing everybody in the social networks how calm and collected you are when criticised, even unfairly. Trust that those who may read the trolls' comments can see who is being reasonable and who is not, remembering that you can't please everybody anyhow. Indeed, I am considering thanking the troll mentioned above for all the free publicity he is giving this book!

Finally, it is obviously important not to become a troll yourself! If you're going to criticise, try to criticise yourself first; if you're going to give praise and congratulations publicly, try to praise and congratulate others, not yourself even indirectly.

As for giving constructive advice or criticisms, try to do so in a private message, not publicly. It is the trolls who seek to prey on the success of others by criticising them publicly; the more successful their target, the better, they believe. Indeed, being trolled can be seen as a sign of your success! They probably wouldn't bother with you, otherwise.

The "competition"

There are those who see their fellow freelance translators as competition. If they discover a great glossary, they keep it secret for their own use instead of sharing it in a forum. They avoid recommending other translators, attempting to do all the work they receive themselves, even if there is too much, for fear of competing translators "stealing" their clients. This not only has a negative effect on themselves and on the profession in general, but also creates its own negative karma. "What goes around, comes around," as they say, and this is certainly true in my experience. As someone who gives work and advice to others, I have found that in general I do indeed get the same treatment back. In fact, I think it has been a fundamental factor in my professional success.

By showing you have some good advice and glossaries, for example, you are also making other translators aware that you're a good translator who knows what they're doing. They may well remember you when they have work you can do.

We are all in the same big boat and there is plenty of work to go around. While some fear the ever-improving machine translation and other forms of translation in the Internet Age, this era has also brought with it a seemingly infinite amount of texts to be translated and proofread by expert humans. There is no shortage of work or clients; we just have to find them and help them see the essential need for our services.

Comparisons

One reason why some people always see others in their profession as "the competition" is that they are constantly comparing themselves to others. On a psychological level, this is a futile exercise since there will always be others who do some things better than you (and worse), no matter how much you learn and improve. In other words, you will never be truly satisfied if you always think you have to do better than others in your field.

There is also the fact that in our profession we live in so many different parts of the world in different socio-economic situations. A translator living in an expensive area of London may be earning twice as much as someone living on a beautiful island in the Philippines, but what of their true standard of living and how far does their money go? Only you can decide how much is a good income for your situation.

That said, there is one healthy comparison we should all make once in a while, and that is to compare yourself to your former self, for example one year ago. Have you improved certain skills? Are you earning more? Do you have better clients? Are you happier? If the answer to any of these questions is "no", you may wish to consider making some changes (and implementing some of the tips in this book!).

Here's another example to illustrate this point:

Once when I was staying in a friend's town I didn't know very well, I decided to keep up my usual jogging routine and asked him about a possible route I could do of a similar distance to my usual route back home. I set out on that route the next morning: round the park, along the country lane, then back along the long avenue lined with identical terraced houses with white doors. Using my mobile app, I checked my time to see if it was more or less the same as on my usual route back home.

The problem began when I realised that there was another jogger who seemed far fitter than me and who seemed to have a similar route here at the same time of morning, so I ended up coinciding with him, which bugged me a little. But then I thought, "If I try to compete with this guy, I'll surely improve!" So for a few days I quietly tried to keep up with him and follow his pace and route. However, he was clearly more professional than me. He even began to tease me, letting me catch up and then sprinting off with a smile on his face.

I finally gave up and began to set myself goals, using markers to pace myself: my number of strides between lampposts and my time on passing the park gates, the peculiar tree in the lane and the solitary black door in the line of white doors along the street near the end of the route. Checking my time as I reached these markers every day, I gradually improved, beating my previous time day after day.

Then one day a strange thing happened. As I was nearing the end of my route, I looked up and realised I was far behind my usual time, with the black door still nowhere in sight. So I picked up my pace and sprinted the last few hundred metres, not wanting to be "beaten" by my former self by running a slower time than I had achieved the day before. I even passed by my erstwhile "competitor", but now paid no attention to him, reaching my own particular, imaginary finishing line, exhausted.

As I stood there panting, the other jogger passed by me and nodded at me, saying "You've improved!"

I looked back down the street and finally it dawned on me: there was no black door. It had finally been painted white to match the others.

But I had only finally beaten the "competition" when I had set my own goals, route and pace.[18]

---

[18] Of course, another simple possibility would have been to ask the better athlete for advice instead of trying to compete with him!

<u>Learning to say "no"</u>

The fear of saying "no" is a common problem that needs to be overcome if we are to progress, as we have mentioned.

I remember hearing about a company that offered exactly the same job in two different ads with little mention of what was required of the applicants. One advertised that it would pay €120,000 a year, and the other €30,000. The lower-paying ad received thousands of applicants, while the higher-paying one got just three. This would seem to suggest that people generally don't value their own work enough. But if you don't ask, you don't get.

In a previous section, I said that we have to learn to say "no" to some clients, whether it's because their fees are too low or the job is a tall order. For whatever reason, some people have problems in doing so. It may be because they fear losing a client, or simply due to a lack of self-esteem. If this is your case, there is a psychological game you can play to help you. Spend a day or week practising saying "no" to your family, friends and people around you in general:

"Can you take the dog for a walk?" "No."

"Do you fancy seeing this film?" "No."

"How about this wine?" "No."

Obviously, you can avoid marital problems by simply saying "yes" a little later if the request is a truly important one! The idea is to get used to the idea of simply saying "no" to things you don't really want to do. Some of us need to realise that this is not the end of the world. It has also been shown to help our ability to be decisive and to go for what we truly want in life.

And of course, if you find it too hard to say "no", try "yeah, but…"

You should not feel that you have "lost" a client if they refuse to pay your reasonable fee because they find it too expensive. On the contrary, you are entitled to think that they have lost you. Once when I was talking with a successful young translator who had set up her own small business that was doing very well, I asked her if there was anything she'd learned that particularly stood out. She said the biggest surprise was when she realised that many customers, particularly big companies, ask for discounts "just because". They don't argue when she doesn't give it to them. In other words, they ask for discounts as standard practice simply to get the best prices whenever possible, not because they realistically expect to get those discounts. But again: if you don't ask, you don't get. They know this. Now, that translator simply states her prices. In her specialisation she doesn't need to back down because there are plenty of needy clients in her sector. When a client doesn't like her fees, she hasn't lost a client; they've lost her.

In order to help the profession generally, you may like to prepare a polite, professional email reply to "bottom-feeding", low-paying potential clients who offer a truly miserable fee. Tell them why their fee is unacceptable. Have this email ready to send almost automatically to such cheapskates.

<u>"Luck"</u>

Luck affects everything. Let your hook always be cast; in the stream where you least expect it there will be a fish.

- Ovid

As with any profession or walk of life, some people seem to be a little luckier than others. However, we shouldn't overestimate this factor or ignore the fact that we can help tip the balance of luck in our favour.

By way of example, here's another anecdote. I have one such friend who everybody thinks is a very lucky man. Everything seems to go his way all the time. However, I know this is not true. In his profession, I know he spent several years abroad in badly-paid jobs to get where he is today. He was also recently divorced. But somehow he exudes an air of serendipity. He's always smiling and joking; generally people are glad to see him. Recently, he had a particularly big piece of luck: a friend of his had won a holiday for two around America, all expenses paid, for three weeks. As the holiday was for two but his friend was also recently divorced, he invited my "lucky" friend on holiday with him.

Most people commented once again on how lucky he had been, not without a little envy. But when I stopped to think about it, I realised that it wasn't only luck. Of course, my friend was fortunate in that a free holiday vacancy had appeared, but the vacancy could have been given to anyone. Why did the man choose my friend as his travelling companion for three weeks?

Anyone who has spent more than a week travelling with another person knows the little tensions that can arise due to different tastes, habits, foibles, etc. So if you won a holiday and had to travel with a companion for three weeks, who would it be? As I pointed out, this friend in particular is a generally very affable, likeable person who's very easy to get on with.

So was it really down to luck that his friend chose him? We all like to travel, live and work with friendly people who do not easily fall into a bad mood. When a lucky break appears, such people are the ones who benefit.

Remember this when answering the phone, commenting in forums, or just having a drink with friends. I myself recently ended up getting a free sailing boat journey across the Mediterranean through a friend I met in a bar one evening when I went out by myself in boredom, whose tales I listened to with genuine interest. I have found translation jobs through people I have met in all kinds of situations by simply having my business cards on me. Nobody ever meets me without discovering that I'm a translator; I make sure of that!

Let your hook always be cast.

Karma chameleons

Over the last few years, a very curious change has taken place in the many congresses I have attended in the EU and Spain. As the economic crisis deepened, I found that the general attitude of the translators and interpreters attending these gatherings actually improved. Why is this?

I remember going to conferences several years ago where the general topics of conversation focussed on the controversial practices of a few infamous agencies and on fees paid to translators and interpreters, which were generally considered to be too low. Many attendees assumed that the few "bad" agencies out there were representative of the profession in general and they also became embroiled in never-ending, bitter arguments about fees. It disheartened me to see so few attendees talking about the undoubted advantages of our profession, enjoying the congress itself, networking (for work and socially) and discussing practical matters to improve their services (CAT tools, associations, courses, specialisations, techniques, news etc.). But as I have said, this seems to have changed. The reason may be that those vociferous, negative attendees have not survived the economic crisis and their own karma.

A few years ago I was asked to give a talk about the business side of translation to a large gathering of translation and interpreting students at a university. As I prepared my presentation, it struck me that ours is a very peculiar profession compared to many others in one respect. Most university students, be they engineers, computer programmers or economists, start sending their résumés to big companies as soon as they graduate or even before, if they do not already have a company post lined up through a scholarship. Most translation and interpreting graduates, however, are condemned to be freelancers or start up their own small business. In other words, being an entrepreneur seems to be part of our job description.

Of course, there are a few big translation multinationals out there and a great many small and medium-sized ones where young professionals can seek an internship as a way of learning the ropes in the "real world". But I find this is a profession where business nous is essential if you are to make a good living. We have no unions, big labour agreements or countless other "privileges" that other professions enjoy. Nonetheless, not wanting to daunt the students who were going to be listening to me, I also emphasised the positive side: vacations more or less when we like, travel opportunities, colleagues all over the world, no glass ceiling, always learning new things...and I soon realised that for me the pros far outweigh the cons. It is surprising, then, that so few congress attendees seemed happy—before the recession.

I pondered the negative comments I had constantly heard from the translation trolls, one of which was the exhausting need to chase up bad payers. Over the years, I myself have only had one client who didn't pay. Actually, he paid most of the invoice, but baulked on an extra, urgent job I had done at the eleventh hour, wrongly claiming to have paid it already. I should stress that this was a direct client, not an agency. An architect, in fact. A world famous architect. In other words, this was a client who could easily have afforded to pay me and save himself legal hassles. Taking into account the fact that this happened in economic boom times, the experience reinforced my belief that bad payers are generally bad payers whatever the economic climate (and the same goes for the good ones). In other words, it seems to have more to do with their character, organisation and professionalism than with external economic pressures. A good payer will always ensure they have the liquidity to cover your work before giving you the job, whether or not their end client finally pays up. As an outsourcer myself sometimes, I apply the same work ethic and common sense. My debt is to the translator who works for me; the payment situation with my end client is my problem and it should not affect my outsourced translator. (I am also to blame if I choose an inadequate translator, so I pay the translator even if they've done a poor job.) Again, since the economic crisis began, I have seen fewer of those late-paying agencies using the excuse that "the end client hasn't paid us yet". You are free to guess why.

Of course, tough economic times bring out the stoic character in most of us, but a stoic attitude can also be a very positive, cheerful one. I try to follow a piece of advice from one of the most renowned stoicists, Marcus Aurelius: "Begin each day by telling yourself: Today I shall be meeting with interference, ingratitude, insolence, disloyalty, ill-will, and selfishness." It sounds pretty negative, yet the effect is positive. If we expect a difficult client, a rude phone call, a troll or a ghastly source text at some time over the coming day, then it doesn't take us by surprise or get us down. Just as Marcus Aurelius also says later in that famous quote, I have found that negative people are generally not happy for some reason in their own personal lives and thus receive my sympathy. Maybe a loved one is ill, they've just got divorced...whatever the reason, by being negative they are not helping themselves and I certainly don't feel offended by them, but rather pity them for being unhappy. And it is certainly true that rudeness and insults do far more damage in the long run to those who proffer them than to those who receive them. (Indeed, I no longer delete nasty comments posted on my social networks since I've realised this fact.) We all want to work with pleasant people.

A famous piece of sales advice perfectly exemplifies this inspiring, positive vibe that one can learn from the quote by the Roman emperor. Imagine you are a door-to-door salesperson or cold caller. The large number of doors shut in your face and phones slammed down every day by irritated potential clients can obviously be depressing. Let's say the statistics are one sale for every hundred calls. That in itself may seem discouraging, but once we have accepted this statistic as a cold fact, we then *expect* to have ninety-nine failed calls before making a sale, and it no longer seems so disappointing or overwhelming. It's just part of the job. One sale per a hundred is a success. In times of economic crisis, this may be one in two hundred, but the principle remains the same.

I have no intention of belittling the situation of those who are having a hard time to make ends meet in this profession; I simply wish to convey the importance of attitude. Moreover, this is not a patronising case of preaching good behaviour, but a practical tip. To illustrate this, let us look at another practical situation. Suppose you have a direct client or agency that is very late on your payment. Aside from legal action and other practical steps, you have two possible options in *the way you react* to the situation — negative or positive:

Negative: You vent your frustration by sending a threatening, rude email demanding your money, labelling your client as unprofessional and incommunicative. You may also do this on a public blacklist or in a forum.

Positive: You write them an email listing your grievances while making no character judgment, giving only the specific facts (deadlines, agreed terms that have been broken, delays in communication etc.). Again, you may decide to do this publicly.

What are the possible outcomes of these two options? Firstly, as we've already seen, it is very important to put ourselves in our client's shoes for a moment before jumping the gun and choosing our reaction. Why is the payment late? Perhaps there is an understandable, justifiable reason. If so and you have simply given the facts without losing your cool, they can then explain the situation (publicly if necessary) with no hard feelings all round. By giving the bad payer the benefit of the doubt, our reaction becomes more positive. Above all, it is important to humanise our clients in the inevitably virtual working environment of the translator; there is always a human on the other side of your screen. So let us look at the outcomes that result from each of the above two options:

Negative: The client may not want to work with you ever again (or other clients if your reaction has been public, on seeing your negative attitude).

Positive: The client may want to work with you again (and others on seeing your positive, calm professionalism).

Let me stress that I am not judging whether you are right or wrong in your reaction. Indeed, you may well be justified in the negative case, particularly if the client really is a rogue. But the important point to note is that the final, long-term outcome depends to an extent on *the way you react* to the situation, not only on the situation itself. A dishonest bad payer may simply never pay, but how that affects you emotionally and your professional image is your decision. Nobody wants to work with a bad-tempered colleague who may one day denounce them publicly if things go wrong.

In short, then, we should ask ourselves: *does the situation affect us or do we affect the situation*? I have found that the translators and interpreters who have weathered the economic storm are the ones who have consciously decided on the latter option. Those colleagues and friends I have made at congresses and seminars over the years and who are still in business are the ones who have never dwelled on acrimonious arguments over fees or dealing with the minority of bad payers who they have usually had the good business sense to avoid. They are the ones with whom I can chat about many other matters related to our work or not, and joke about our bad experiences and the good lessons we have learned from them.

With the social networks, forums and associations, we have the opportunity to get into arguments about fees and "bottom-feeding", disreputable clients that will unfortunately always exist in any profession. Or we have the opportunity to find some understanding ears, advice on a myriad of matters, or simply to joke about our tough times with those who've also been there.

That choice is yours alone.

Thoughts on Translation

A Bridge Too Far: Politics and Journalism

Though our clients may sometimes seem unaware of it, as translators we know that no matter how much machine translation improves, one attribute it will never match is our very human ability to connect with the source and target audience, both intellectually and empathetically. This connection is precisely what allows us to adapt the original message to achieve the best results for the client. For instance, we understand that even though the author and the target audience live in the same geographic area, they could still be separated by vast social and cultural differences. As such, conveying the intended message successfully requires the translator to bridge these differences in the text. How? Through our in-depth knowledge of various aspects of the target readers, such as their sense of humour, register, professional practices and even social sensitivities. This insight will go a long way towards avoiding disastrous results for the author/client by getting the message across as tactfully, eloquently and clearly as possible. Perhaps one of the most striking examples of this linguistic and cultural minefield that is our daily bread and butter is to be found in one of my own fields of specialisation: politics in Spain.

Nation, country or state?

First, let me give a very brief description of the scenario in which I sometimes work, which can involve conveying the same message in a tactful manner to different political affiliations. As a translator from both Catalan and Spanish, my direct and indirect clients sometimes include both national Spanish and regional Catalan bodies. As an example of the pitfalls this presents, the sentence you have just read may well be considered offensive by many readers. This is because I referred to Catalonia as a region, not a country. Such an apparently innocent statement may be perfectly acceptable to most readers living in another part of Spain or the world. However, the same statement might be quite offensive to those living in Catalonia, particularly if they work in the government and are sensitive to the political loyalties of potential voters and patriotic citizens. Such is the importance of knowing who is going to read the text eventually, as well as who is paying for the translation. If I say that Catalonia is simply a region of Spain, my Catalan client might not be at all happy. Nevertheless, if the target English-speaking reader knows nothing of Spanish geography or politics, I must somehow explain what Catalonia *is* in the translation.

So, using the example above as a starting point, what is Catalonia exactly? Such an apparently simple question may provide a wide variety of answers depending on whom you ask (the client, the reader, the author, etc.). To a patriotic Catalan, it is without a doubt a country. To an equally patriotic Spaniard, it is without a doubt a region. Spain itself and the Spanish government are referred to by most politically correct Catalans as simply the "State". Obviously, to a reader in the U.S., this word brings to mind one of 50 autonomous regions, which is generally what a typical non-Catalan Spaniard would understand Catalonia to be— an autonomous region. This leads us back to square one. By now you are probably beginning to see the quandary.

Of course, it all boils down to what each person means when using the word *country*. The UK is a nation made up of various countries. Then there are unofficial regions within it that are known as countries (e.g. the Black Country, named after its coal mines). As a *country* is an invented, abstract human concept, its significance varies according to each human who reads, hears or uses it depending on the context and the person's own beliefs (such as patriotism or lack of it). It is necessary to know if the word has legal and political ramifications in the context in which it is used (e.g. England and Scotland) or not (e.g. the Black Country). If we wish to be specific, the word *nation*, for example, is usually the one that refers to a legal entity with borders, armed forces and a government that can collect taxes and take binding legal decisions over the population within its borders (e.g. the UK). It is usually understood also as a *state*, though this word has other interpretations. In any case, when using all such words and their translations, one must be aware of their significance for the target population.

Language or dialect?

The Catalan language is also spoken in the Valencia region on the eastern *Levante* coast of Spain and in the Balearic Islands, albeit with different dialects. Once again, here is another statement that might cause offence. If you ask the Valencians, they may well tell you that they actually speak a different language called Valencian, while the islanders may tell you they speak a language known as Majorcan. (Majorcan can itself be referred to by other names depending on the island.) In fact, such sensitivity has led some documents in Europe and Spain to refer to what is essentially the same language in politically correct yet linguistically clumsy terms, such as: "Catalan, which is known as Valencian in the Valencia territory, and Majorcan in the Balearic Islands." This kind of diplomatic chicanery should keep everybody happy but the reader, who simply wishes to get some concise, direct information.

So, when is a language not a language? The short answer is: when it is a dialect. And here we enter another political minefield. Ask a linguist what the difference is between Catalan and Valencian, and he or she will most probably tell you that they are essentially the same language with some minor differences—in other words, two dialects of the same language. But as is usually the case in any part of the world, when we ask a politician such a simple question, the answer may vary wildly. Many Catalan politicians will tell you that both Catalan and Valencian are one language (and they will call it Catalan). Most Valencians, however, will call the language they speak Valencian, and may even tell you it is a language separate from Catalan. Again, this will depend on their nationalistic and political tendencies (e.g., pro-Spanish, pro-Catalan, pro-Valencian, nationalist, anti-nationalist or couldn't-care-less).

While many Valencian politicians and public institutions consider their local tongue to be a separate language, they have not been successful in convincing linguists, official international bodies and legal institutions that it is more than a dialect. For example, when Spain was required to have its constitution translated into all of its official languages and deliver copies to the institutions of the European Union before holding a referendum on the EU Constitution, some of the European delegates were baffled to find that the Valencian and Catalan copies were virtually identical.

You may be thinking that translations between Catalan and Valencian would lead to a large number of fuzzy matches due to the many similarities in both vocabulary and grammar, and you would be right. In fact, most linguists agree that Catalan and Valencian are indeed dialects of the same language. Unfortunately for translators and patriotic Valencians, the International Assigned Numbers Authority has decided that the two "languages" merit just one language code for translation memories, etc.: CA (which presumably stands for *Catalan*).[19] Furthermore, in my own experience the call for such translations is virtually nil. I have never heard of a translator being asked to "translate" from Catalan into Valencian or vice versa. Such a "translation" would more likely be considered a "correction", "adaptation" or "revision", particularly by Catalans "correcting" from Valencian into Catalan.

One also has to consider that most Catalan speakers, and some purportedly politically correct Spaniards, generally refer to Spanish as *Castellà* (Castilian). This is a wide generalisation that associates the Spanish language with its geographical roots of Castile, thereby avoiding associating it with the entire territory of Spain (which would include Catalonia), even though it is indeed the only official language covering the whole of Spain (including Catalonia).[20]

The level of sensitivity in naming a language varies enormously around the globe, often depending on the local historical and social background. As far as I know, there are no citizens in the USA who feel offended because their official language is called English

---

[19] The International Assigned Numbers Authority is responsible for coordinating some of the key elements that keep the internet running smoothly. Specifically, it allocates and maintains unique codes and numbering systems that are used in the technical standards ("protocols") that drive the internet. For more information, see www.iana.org.

[20] Catalan is a co-official language, along with Spanish, in Catalonia, Valencia and the Balearic Islands. It is widely used as an everyday language throughout these territories and Andorra, and as a medium of instruction in many schools (nearly all schools in Catalonia). It is also used extensively in the local media and government.

(as opposed to North American, for example). Given the history of England and the USA, they could certainly find justifications to avoid using the etymological reference to their past imperialist rulers.

Country or region?

Geographical terminology can also vary depending upon whom you ask. Catalans generally refer to their own territory as a country and to the Valencia area as the "Valencian country." In fact, both the Valencia area and the islands are often known by Catalans as the "Catalan countries," which many in said regions find offensive, as they may not want to consider their land to be a mere extension of Catalonia. They are mostly happy to call themselves Spanish and their country Spain. The Valencians themselves, on the other hand, mostly refer to their own region as an "Autonomous Community region" (the translation is an overly literal calque). They refer to Catalonia in similar terms (an autonomous region of Spain), which the generally more patriotic Catalans find equally offensive, as they consider their land to be a country in itself, not merely part of another.

In the end, since those who will be reading my translations reside both in and outside of Spain, I tend to follow a policy of simply getting the message across as succinctly and clearly as possible. Sometimes I might feel it necessary to acknowledge my clients' patriotic leanings by providing an explanation in parentheses the first time sensitive expressions appear. For example, if I am translating a text written by Catalans for an English-speaking audience unaware of Spanish geography and politics, the first time the text refers to Catalonia as a country I might say: "throughout the region (the country of Catalonia)," or " … throughout the country (region of Spain)." One can also resort to translator's footnotes. As my backup in the face of potential client complaints, I may turn to official lists such as those from the European Union or UN (*http://ow.ly/4mR9Hw* and *http://bit.ly/eF7pno*) or even examples used previously (or noticeably omitted) in the past by the same organisations in official texts or laws (e.g., http://eur-lex.europa.eu). Another possibility is to make a note of the terms generally used in articles and reports in internationally renowned media such as the BBC, *The Economist* or *The New York Times*.

A far simpler option, of course, is to omit the word "region" or "country" altogether in the target text (e.g., simply put "Spain" or "Catalonia"). While the UN may officially refer to a country as the Democratic People's Republic in order to avoid displeasing said country's political representatives, depending on our target readers we may simply decide to call it North Korea in a general text to avoid treading on anybody's sensitive toes.

Racism?

Of course, we need to be aware of cultural perceptions of what is offensive or not. For example, there is no accurate translation of the dreaded, racist "N" word into some languages and cultures, though this does not mean that racism does not exist within them. In many Hispanic cultures, the idea of parodying other races' traits (physical appearance, foreign accents) is sometimes perceived and intended as non-racist, harmless fun. However, your clients should be aware of the danger of doing so in English-speaking cultures, for example. There was the infamous case of the Spanish national basketball team's photo for the Olympic games in China, with the entire team making "Chinese eyes" by stretching their eyes with their forefingers. Other countries were appalled, whilst the Spanish media were rather perplexed at the reaction, which they felt to be excessive. They saw the gesture as a fond one towards their Chinese hosts.

Translating politics

When it comes to politics, there are times when it is humanly impossible to avoid offending someone; when the cultural, religious, or political chasm is simply too wide to bridge. It is a sad fact of life that some people can be generally offensive, and others easily offended. It may even be ethically wrong of us to attempt to soften a message, as this in itself is a manipulation of the source text (or voice). As in any translation job, we need to be aware at all times of who the author and potential readers are, as well as the author's intent. (This applies to our reference sources, too. A brief look at the Wikipedia articles about Gibraltar or the Falkland Islands in Spanish and English shows that our sources may vary wildly.)

Ask yourself if it is really your job to be acting as a diplomat. If you are not sure, you should simply check that the client and the author are aware of the effect their text is going to have on the end readers. This means consulting with them and offering possible alternatives to the original wording. Another option is to create a "political" glossary for each client's preferences. In the examples above, this could include each client's preferred country/region/language names, for example. You may even decide to refuse the job if the opinions and expressions used are offensive to you personally.

No doubt there are other intricate linguistic hotspots around the globe where the translator must go to great lengths to avoid stepping on the political toes of clients and readers. I would go as far as to say that the world's greatest diplomats are indeed those who are reading this book—translators and interpreters. All of you in your different areas of specialisation come across your own challenges of bridging the cultural divide for your clients, who mostly remain blissfully unaware of the knowledge, thought, and imagination necessary to convey their messages seamlessly from one language into another, and from one culture into another. However, it is precisely this human skill that makes your work so essential. Clients who ignore this fact do so at their peril.

Word Crunching: Thoughts on Machine Translation

Everybody now knows about Google Translate, including our clients. Clearly, this can create suspicions about whether human translators are truly necessary and how we are helped by computer aided translation (CAT) tools. From a translator's point of view, we have to accept that machine translation (MT) is here to stay; we ignore it at our peril. Let's look briefly at the pros and cons.

One advantage of MT is that there is less human error in the sense of copying numbers and dates from the source to the target text (though good use of CAT tools can also cover this aspect). On the other hand, the machine may translate "untranslatables"— proper nouns such as brand names and people's names. Machine translation is also much faster, yet prone to big mistakes due to its inability to account for the target readers and their culture. There are things that simply should not be translated to avoid offending people, for example. It can hardly be expected to deal with such human traits as metaphors, puns and newly invented words, either.

The machine translator's great speed has led some to believe that our job will become more one of proofreading machine-translated texts as opposed to translating them ourselves. Indeed, there are some agencies that already use this controversial method to keep prices down (and possibly the quality, too). However, as we have seen, it is necessary to know much more about the target readers and their culture to avoid big mistakes, as well as seeing the original source text to make sure the target text really does reflect it. In other words, it can take the same or longer to proofread a machine-translated text than to do a human translation from scratch, with more possibility of mistakes appearing in the former. We have before us a very interesting example of mankind vs. machine in a battle of intelligence, but our clients must never forget that the texts are written by and for humans. The translator in between should therefore also be human to avoid unhuman error.

Monte-Carlo number-crunching methods have long been used as a comparable "brute" method of finding mathematical answers. A classic example may be Deep Blue's seemingly infinite "random paths" for deciding the best possible next chess move when pitted against Gary Kasparov. I suspect many scientists were hoping the computer would win, especially those who created the digital beast, but most humans probably had a secret desire to see the human come out triumphant. In fact, the Russian did win one match and drew three, but lost two. So few results are statistically insignificant, but obviously Kasparov, with the "disadvantage" of being human, was unable to generate billions of potential moves like his opponent and yet was capable of winning. How was this possible? I believe the answer, and the analogy, can be applied to machine translation.

Let's look at how machine translation works, taking Google Translate as an example. With the astronomical amount of words passing through their servers every day, they certainly have a lot of words to crunch through their translation software. By a process of choosing the mode, that is to say the "most used word" on the internet, the machine is able to choose what it considers the most likely translation for a specific word by comparing and aligning texts in different languages. (Incidentally, take a good read of the policy regulations before setting up a mail account with such large internet service providers and you'll understand why you shouldn't send both your source and translated texts via these – you may simply be adding to the company's huge translation memories. And when it comes to confidential texts, you must not let these be used by third parties such as these service providers via their MT.) This is not so different from the most widely used dictionaries in the world conducting surveys to see how many people use a word before officially accepting it in their dictionaries. However, there are two problems with this, where we human translators can undoubtedly outwit the machine just like Kasparov. Firstly, the machine trips up with exceptions (Kasparov did the *unexpected* by not always choosing the "best" move) and with poetic licence. The metaphor, for example, can derail it. Secondly, there are very often words that are used among professionals such as doctors and engineers that have a synonym which is far more commonly used by the general public (and which the machine may therefore choose as the most probable translation). This is an obvious example where we need a human translator to understand who is writing the text, its purpose, who it is for and the general and specific contexts in which it is being used. (It should be noted, nevertheless, that Google Translate is improving in terms of identifying the context and concordance of words in a given sentence. The more context (i.e. text) it receives, the more accurate it is, but also the more possibilities for making mistakes with "unexpected" words.)

Clearly, we human translators must take enormous care in using such tools, and always only as an aid. For example, after translating a text you may find it useful to run a few words (never the whole text) through to see what words the computer chooses and give you some new ideas that may not have occurred to you, rather like a thesaurus. But even in this case, one should never forget that the mode (average best answer) may not always be correct. One has only to look at the examples in human history of landslide majorities voting for thuggish dictators to realise that the majority can often be wrong. Just because a word is used more frequently does not mean it is correct; one has to check the official sources and consider the specific context. There is also the threat of plagiarism; a scientific author with a new patent will not be pleased to find their closely guarded secret floating around a famous search engine's TM. The same consideration must be made with confidential legal texts and personal information, for example.

You must not let third parties process such documents via MT, for example.

As far as clients' use of machine translators such as Google Translate is concerned, it is our job to remind them that the end reader is a human, not a machine, with all of the cultural complexities and issues that this implies.

Computers can also be used to intelligently "generate" their own literature. In his classic book *Fooled by Randomness*, Nassim Nicholas Taleb tells of how he used Andrew C. Bulhak's Dada Engine to come up with phrases like this: "It could be said that if cultural narrative holds, we have to choose between the dialectic paradigm of narrative and neoconceptual Marxism. Sartre's analysis of cultural narrative holds that society, paradoxically, has objective value." Such pseudo-intellectual drivel may sound familiar to anyone who has translated for low-brow art critics.

Then we have the tantalising prospect of machine interpreting, which may not be so far-fetched as many still believe. Whenever you talk on the phone, your voice is digitised before reaching the receiver, and this has been so for many years now. It's not your mother you hear, it's a computer copying her. A computer can "learn" an individual human's voice and reproduce it with new sentences of its own. The *Terminator* films may start to ring a bell. This may be old hat to James Bond or the CIA, which leads one to think that the next step can now be taken. In fact, the BBC and others seem to be well on the way to doing it, albeit unwittingly. The corporation has been using live subtitling for years now. To do so, one may either employ an extremely fast typist or, you guessed it, a computer. Basically, the computer recognises the voice and flashes the words it has understood onto the screen. From what I have seen, I'd say it gets over 90 % right, which in my opinion is quite impressive, especially when faced with so many accents. Imagine a Glaswegian interviewee saying "I cannae. D'you see?

D'you ken?" The machine may well understand this to mean "A can o' juicy chicken," for example. However, this hiccup can also be overcome. After crunching thousands of interview samples in Glasgow, the computer has only to be told *where* or *who* it is translating to get the gist. Taking another leap forward, GPS could also be employed to automatically inform the computer when it is in Glasgow or Los Angeles, so it can adjust its voice recognition and vocabulary accordingly.

This is how the hand-held mobile phone interpreter can be made to work better. Nevertheless, the same drawbacks apply as with machine translation. If you are asked by an angry-looking punk rocker with a blue Mohican and a padlock through their nose late at night in a dark alley, asking "What are you looking at?" the answer should be a lie or best left unspoken.

Six reasons why humans translate better than machines

Clients who know little about translation are often convinced that machine translation is almost as good as human translation. This is clearly a misconception we need to dispel in order to produce a good translation, maintain the good name of the profession and keep up our human fees.

To help you do so, below you can find a list of six very good reasons why humans will always translate better than machines (until artificial intelligence is truly achieved, perhaps).

One:

Humans read between and behind the lines.

(What is the author's intent?)

"What did you think of our report?"

"It's OK, I guess."

Depending on the human source and target cultures, this reply can be construed to have very different meanings. If it comes from a British person, "OK, I guess" is actually less than lukewarm. It could really mean "It's not at all OK, but I don't want to hurt your feelings so I'm being diplomatic. We need to talk."

Likewise, a Japanese business email may drag on for twenty lines of pleasantries in which the actual message lies buried, whereas a hard-headed business executive from Singapore will want the email to get straight to the point and would find such an email tiresome and impractical. A human translator can understand this and adapt the message accordingly.

Two:

MT is digital; humans are analogue.

(Does the text "flow"?)

One area in which it still seems universally accepted that humans do best is in post-editing, one of the last inspections of the text before it reaches its intended readers. A simple example of why this is so can be found in the matter of translation software segments.

Let's say a paragraph of six sentences has been neatly translated sentence-by-sentence and thus divided into six such neat chunks now known as "translation segments", easily handled by a machine. On the final review, the human translator may decide to use a different sentence order and completely re-arrange the paragraph to make more logical sense in the target readers' culture. Or they may decide to chop up one or two gigantic, meandering sentences into smaller, more digestible phrases. On the other hand, they may prefer to join two or three short, stuttering sentences into a longer, flowing one. Such stylistic decisions are still the domain of the human translator and will be for a long time to come.

Three:

Machines don't get culture shock.

(Will this bikini ad work in Saudi Arabia?)

As all diplomats know, sometimes in human communication the best thing to say is nothing at all. Languages are born out of cultures with all of their historical human baggage: humour, gender roles, work ethic, religion, concepts of justice, family roles, political and judicial systems, manners, taboos, etc. A human translator will ring the alarm bell if they see an erotic ad or hear a sexist joke intended for an audience with whom it will go down like a lead balloon. Machines just translate.

Nevertheless, it should be said that perhaps in this case the machine is at least more honest. In a perfect world, maybe the translation should be allowed to go ahead with all of its disastrous consequences, so the reader truly understands the author. But in the real world the customer is not always right, which is why they need a human translator to correct them.

Four:

Human writers make mistakes; computers don't.

(And that's why human translators are more reliable.)

A common shortcoming of translation courses is that they invariably use perfect source texts for students to practise translating. In the real world, texts that are yet to be translated and published are hardly ever free of mistakes of all kinds; not just punctuation and spelling errors, but dodgy factual information, wrong vocabulary usage or simply tired writers' lapses. There may even be intentionally poor or ambiguous wording from a wily lawyer or else texts by authors who are simply not good at writing because it's not their job, such as engineers or hurried doctors with their infamous shorthand. Human translators—and particularly those who have worked in professional fields other than translation—understand this and spot such human mistakes that the computer doesn't notice, precisely because it isn't human.

Furthermore, the fact that human translators can also tactfully point out mistakes to the author and offer alternatives is another service the computer doesn't provide. This leads us to yet another advantage we have over machines…

Five:

Humans ask human questions.

(What's the text for?)

Is the text for children or the elderly? Specialist doctors or their patients? Mexicans or Spaniards? Jews, Muslims or atheists?

Hilarious or deadly serious? Is it advertising a product to sell it or simply providing practical public information about it? Will that ad campaign work as well in China as it does in the USA? If not, perhaps it needs re-thinking and re-writing from scratch ("transcreation"), in which case your translator has just saved your company some heavy losses simply by pointing that out.

Six:

Humans write the message and humans read the message.

(So who should be in the middle? Well, duh.)

Texts are written by humans to be read by humans. But if the writers and their intended readers work in different languages, the text has to be translated. So will a machine or a human best understand and translate a text written with human intent for human effect? Well, duh. The true test of artificial intelligence is not whether a machine can "fake" human interaction, but whether it can actually "do" it. It is one thing to translate *Macbeth*; quite another to write it.

Human translators write.

People Crunching: Thoughts on Crowd Translation

Aside from the ethical questions of whether people should work for peanuts or free for large corporations, how effective is crowd translation?

Perhaps we need to consider this question since it is a growing phenomenon that our potential clients may be tempted to use. Again, there is the same fallacy inherent in statistical machine translation that "the more people and brains work on a project, the better the results". Needless to say, this is easily refuted. Just because a thousand people work on designing a bridge or a building, they will not do a better job than a single qualified civil engineer or architect. Or put simply, too many (unqualified or inexperienced) cooks can spoil the broth.

Would your client prefer a thousand law students to work on their contract and trial, or a small but experienced, qualified professional team of lawyers? Would you let several medical students operate on you instead of a qualified, experienced surgeon?

The question of consistency must also be taken into account. Again, this should be remembered if a non-LSP client tries to get a team of translators together to translate a large text or the same text into several languages. Only professionals know the importance of consistency in the terminology and how to handle it.

Point this out to the client.

Small Interpreting Jobs

What kind of interpreting job can you do?

Interpreting (spoken translation) is an entire profession in itself. If you are serious about becoming an interpreter to make a living, you should consider getting qualified with perhaps a master's degree, for example. However, though you may not be a qualified or experienced professional interpreter, you may get called on from time to time by a client to interpret because you work in a specific field or know the client and their situation well (for example, when meeting with company lawyers to discuss contracts that you have translated).

For such simple liaisons involving simultaneous interpreting, there are a few practical tips we can keep in mind for the job to go relatively smoothly.

As with translation, the client needs to know above all that not just anybody can do a good job of interpreting. In conference interpreting, the interpreter needs to know how to use the equipment and the unwritten rules of such work when accompanied by another interpreter, for example. There should be two interpreters for this kind of work, especially if it is going to last a few hours, so the client has to budget for four hours of interpreting work for every two hours of speech. If for some reason this is impossible given the circumstances, then they should be warned that you will need to take breaks.

Clients should also take into account travel time and costs, overnight stays and other such overheads.

When the job is specialised, as is often the case, the interpreter will also need to brush up on the terminology before the job. This is why a half-day job does not simply cost half the price of a full day, but takes into account the preparation you will have to do.

Talking of which, the client needs to know that you will need time to prepare for the big day. You cannot be expected to talk about nuclear physics one day and cattle farming the next without getting your glossaries ready, etc.

On the day itself, you also need to be assertive in making it clear that you are there to interpret and not to do other little tasks your client or others may ask of you such as handing out papers or carrying something. Use your discretion, but the job you are being paid for is interpreting. Be clear on this so they take you and the profession seriously.

<u>Liaison interpreting tips</u>

As with translation, you can be your client's cultural consultant and adviser when dealing with people from another country. You may also find you need to defend your client in certain situations (for example, if you find that a doctor or lawyer is ignoring them or doing something against their will or cultural/religious norms). You should warn third parties beforehand if you are going to translate everything they say, even if not intended for your client. Likewise, you can simply point out to your client that others are not saying anything important if you see that your client is getting a little agitated at not being able to understand everything in certain situations.

There are times when you may need to change register on interpreting medical or legal jargon for an immigrant with a low level of education, for example. Beware of the client's friends or family trying to take over the job of interpreting with disastrous results, too.

It may also be necessary to be aware of current affairs as well as general culture, particularly if something significant has happened in one of the countries of those you are going to be interpreting for. This could even be something simple like a sporting event or a local public transport strike that's in the news. You never know what may come up, especially if you are going to be liaising all day and having a meal with them, for example.

Talking of which, if your clients go for a meal you should not really be eating, but speaking. Make sure you take some kind of snack with you for the day, and especially a bottle of water. Along with this, you should carry some small items of personal hygiene with you such as a small tube of toothpaste and brush, and perhaps even a small deodorant. You do not know for sure if the job may go on longer than expected or under what physical conditions. This is not a job you can do in your pyjamas! Your image should be in keeping with the professionals and situation you are going to be working with.

Other items you should have with you include a notebook and more than one pen, plus a photocopy with a glossary of terms that may come up in this specific job. Preferably, you should have a laptop or at least a tablet or big smart phone with the relevant glossaries and an internet connection to check unexpected terminology.

If you have the opportunity to take notes in consecutive interpreting, do so. It may well be essential.

There are certain key factors to remember if your notes are truly going to aid your memory.

First, we need to break down the section of speech we have just heard into its important points. We then summarise these, giving them memorable labels. There are some well-known aids to memory for giving such labels.

The important thing to note in using memory aids is that the more outlandish the example you use, the more easily it will stick in your mind.

For example, if the speaker is talking about pros and cons, you could possibly conjure up an image of angels and devils in your head to represent each point, or cheery and depressed people. You can also try to match the discourse to a visual storyboard in your head that follows the logical sequence of the speech. Some people use the idea of a route they know well or the rooms of their house, "placing" parts of the discourse at each memorable stage in the route or room in the house, for example.

For note taking, it is essential to note down numbers and names, as these will be the most difficult to remember, unless they simply form part of a list given as an example, in which case you can just jot down the first few. If you are working with a colleague, the person who is not interpreting at that moment can note down such points to help you.

Certain other parts of speech must be noted down, too, such as connector words (e.g. *however, therefore, despite, in addition, but…*). Use a simple symbol for each of these that you can remember. Your symbols and abbreviations must be unmistakable and well known to you before you begin interpreting the session.

Some more concepts whose symbols you must be ready to jot down are: auxiliary verbs (and other significant parts of speech in other languages), tenses (e.g. a line above the verb to indicate the future, a wiggly line to indicate a conditional), people (e.g. president), a country, important/emphasised points and positive or negative points.

There are many examples of note-taking symbols for interpreters to be found on the internet (see EU links: http://ow.ly/YEEKM), but the important thing is for the symbols to be easily recognisable and memorable for you. If you invent one that works for you, then that's the one you should use.

You will need a notepad with a ring binder or at least one whose pages can easily be turned, preferably bound at the top. The larger the better, provided you are comfortable with it. Generally, it has been found that it's easier to write your thoughts diagonally from the top left to the bottom right of the page within three imaginary vertical columns in which to put your notes/symbols in a logical order. This allows for other symbols to be added later if necessary (for example, if the speaker then refers back to these points, you can just draw an arrow back to them). You can mark a line to show the end of a significant part of speech or thoughts. It is important to only take notes when you have fully understood what has been said, not as you hear it, since this can impede your ability to remember your notes when you come to read them out later.

When interpreting among people, it is important to maintain eye contact with your interlocutors so they can see you're paying attention and have understood, etc. You can also use your gaze and body language to indicate if they're going too fast, etc. and nod to show you've understood and are ready to provide the translation. Avoid hesitating or making long pauses with "errrmm…" as this will cause a feeling of insecurity among your interlocutors as you appear to be unsure. If you need time, it is better to remain silent and make out that you are pausing for effect! (Even Barack Obama appears to have been advised to do this over the years of his presidency.) In a similar vein, you should begin and end your "speech" with a firm tone of voice and perhaps a discourse marker. This gives the impression of a well-rounded sentence in much the same way as a capital letter marks the start of a sentence and a full-stop/period at the end.

As you read back from your notes out loud, try to stay ahead. You should already be looking at the next page of your notes while finishing reading the previous one.

Above all, try to maintain your composure whatever happens, using a steady tone of voice that conveys confidence to reassure the interlocutors.

Finally, you could send your client a copy of *Interpreting, Getting it Right*, available from the American Translators Association:

https://www.atanet.org/publications/getting_it_right_int.pdf

This should guide them through the process avoiding potential pitfalls.

Links for interpreters

General skills

EU interpreting: http://ow.ly/YEEKM

Information about interpreting: studies, techniques, bibliography

http://interpreters.free.fr/

Video material for practising (note-taking)

EU Speech Repository:

www.multilingualspeeches.tv/scic/portal/index.html

Speechpool:

www.speechpool.net

Speeches of the University of Geneva (for students):

http://live.eti.unige.ch/

Videos of conferences at the European Commission (on EU-topics):

http://europa.eu/media-centre/videos-photos/index_en.htm

London School of Economics (webstreamed lectures):

http://www2.lse.ac.uk/newsAndMedia/videoAndAudio/Home.aspx

UN webcast:

www.un.org/webcast/

TED conferences

www.ted.com

Interpreting blogs and websites

www.bootheando.com/

www.theinterpreterdiaries.com/

www.lourdesderioja.com/

www.aiic.net/

Starting Out in Freelance Translation

ProZ.com etc.

If you are an absolute beginner in the translation job market, one website that you will undoubtedly come across and which may help you get started is ProZ.com. This is essentially a huge market place for translation and interpreting service providers and sellers. (Note: it is *not* an agency (or an NGO), nor should you expect it to behave like one. As a market place, you will find a wide range of quality on offer. ProZ.com does make an effort to maintain minimum standards by banning bad payers, posting scam alerts and suggesting minimum fees, for example, but in the end there will always be a minority of scallywags who try to find a way around these so you should have your wits about you as in any market.[21].) Here you will find resources, job offers, training webinars, discounts on tools and forums for help among fellow translators around the world.

There is also a section for asking and answering terminology questions, for which you are rewarded points known as *Kudoz* if your answer is chosen by the asker and your peers as the correct one, which may help your rating on the site, for example. (Note: Again, nothing is perfect and this system is not infallible. It may be prone to a little backslapping by friends who award each other

---

[21] If you do spot truly suspicious cases of malpraxis, notify the ProZ.com staff or moderators who will generally try to act as it is also in their interest to maintain the good name of the website.

points, for example.[22] So, if you look up a word in the Kudoz archives, make sure you look at all the possible entries given the context and any reference material and links that other translators have posted there. The latter can indeed be helpful.)

While some translators complain of some low fees and agencies of supposed ill repute on some sites one must remember that in any business there is a market place where you will find all kinds of translators, outsourcers and agencies of varying size, quality and specialist fields. There is good and bad, users and a few abusers, just as you can find good and bad in Google, Facebook, Twitter and any other well-known internet giant, even though the general services they provide are undoubtedly useful. The ProZ.com website has directories to look up translators' opinions of agencies (the Blue Board) and tries to warn and stay abreast of possible scammers etc. But as said above, it is not infallible nor can it be; in the end you must have your wits about you as in any internet-based freelance profession or indeed any market in the real world. As a complete beginner in freelance translation, you may decide to accept relatively low fees at first anyhow simply to get some practice, not to make a living. (Your resident country's tax and social security systems may also allow you to work part-time or simply pay tax and social security on the relatively small amount of work you do at first.) As you improve your skills and get an idea of how much you need to earn to make a decent living, you can gradually raise your fees (changing clients if necessary) to a respectable level. Over time, you may reach the point where you stop looking at job offers here but decide to maintain your profile etc. for the SEO the ProZ.com website gives you, discounts on

---

[22] See previous footnote.

tools, etc. You will also find that direct clients and agencies who look for you here (as opposed to you looking for them and offering your CV) generally pay better, since they have taken the time and effort to match the job to a suitable translator. Those who simply give their job to the lowest bidder, for example, may not be too worried about quality or paying you well.

ProZ.com also holds in-person congresses and local translator gatherings known as *powwows* (you may even organise your own to get to know your local colleagues in person). There are also glossaries and other tools you may find useful. Although it is free to join and participate in ProZ.com, if you pay about €116.00/year[23] you'll have access to more services, discounts on software and other tools that will give your business a boost. Remember: there is a big difference between *spending* and *investing* money.

There is now a plethora of other sites where you can find work such as TranslatorsCafe.com, like a cheaper, less diverse copy of ProZ.com, with fewer services and generally very low fees paid by the agencies and outsourcers. There are sites like GoTranslators.com, TranslationDirectory.com and many weird and wonderful (or not) web platforms, forums and ideas for finding work. The average fees paid in some such sites can be rather low; I only advise them to start out in the translation business and get some practice to see if this is for you. As your business grows and you get to know other translators, agencies and direct clients, you should have less and less need for intermediaries to find work (though ProZ.com can still be useful to you for the other reasons

---

[23] In early 2016.

mentioned above). Indeed, direct clients are where there is truly good money to be made if you aim at the right market, though these can still find you if you stand on the shoulders of giants. (SEO is another reason why I am still a paying member of ProZ.com; although I no longer actively look for work in the site, clients can find me there.)

CAT tools

With so many pictures of furry pets in some translation fora, you may be mistaken for thinking that our feline friends help with our work, but when translators talk about CAT tools they are actually referring to something quite different. Almost all translators apart from some literary and journalistic translators use Computer Aided Translation tools these days. What are they and what do they do?

Well, very basically, a CAT tool memorises each segment of text you translate in a Translation Memory (TM), so that if you come across a similar segment of text, the tool can recognize it as a "fuzzy match" (i.e. a partial match with a segment of text you have already translated). Using this, you thus only have to make slight changes to adapt the new segment to the current context. This may be particularly useful in rather repetitive texts such as contracts or certain technical manuals, where some paragraphs may be very similar in different texts. For example, if you have ever bothered to read website data protection policies, disclaimers and copyright texts, you'll know that they all say pretty much the same thing. It is basically only the names that change. Unfortunately, some agencies demand discounts for such repetitions. It is up to you whether or not to accept them (taking into account that you will still have to proofread the text in the new context).

Such tools also allow you to build up glossaries etc. for particular clients or subjects, so that the software can immediately identify key terminology in future texts and notify you. Thus, you can maintain coherence and consistency in your texts for particular clients and specialisations. It's also particularly useful for those clients who only need you a few times a year, so you don't have to pore through the old translations to remember that client's specific vocabulary. You can see a succinct explanation here: www.youtube.com/watch?v=wWnfexNYsyI.

The most famous CAT tools on the market today are probably SDL Trados, MemoQ and Wordfast. You can find an overview of these on the ProZ.com website here: www.ProZ.com/software-comparison-tool/cat/cat_tools/2.

Aside from the essential CAT tools, there is other very useful software for translators such as alignment tools (to align texts in different languages, matching paragraphs and sentences, often also included in CAT software), OCR (Optical Character Recognition software, to convert PDFs and scanned documents into Word files, such as ABBYY, ReadIris and OmniPage), word count tools (to count words in PDF and other formats so you can give your client an estimated fee), extraction software (to extract text from websites, for example) and tools for post-editing, automatic billing, project management, quality control, formatting, etc. A quick look and enquiry in translation forums will soon reveal many kinds and recommendations for you to choose from, and some of the above tools may be included in the CAT software itself.

But don't get too carried away. Remind wary clients that CAT tools are not the same as machine translation and the *texts are always written and read by humans, so the go-between who translates them must also be human* to avoid mistakes (context, social norms, etc.) that a machine cannot possibly grasp. And you should not become over-reliant on the tool and its memory. In your target language, maybe two sentences will flow better than one, for example.

Another tool that many translators now use is voice recognition software to avoid physical strain from typing. The most famous one is Dragon Naturally Speaking by Nuance. If you work with English, it may be worth buying another language version since they usually come with English as a default anyhow; that way you will be able to use it in more than one language. You may be surprised at just how advanced and fast this software is today. It can be used to carry out all the commands you need. The days of the keyboard and mouse may well be numbered.

Payment

Each country has its tax and social security laws. You will have to look into your own to see how to become self-employed and above all get a European VAT number if you are an EU citizen.

Many agencies and clients will first send you a P.O. (Purchase Order). This indicates the job you are to do, the deadline and the fee to be paid, as well as billing details you can then put on the invoice. It is the official proof that the client is asking you for the service.

For billing, your invoice should have the following information:

- An invoice number (you can decide on this or ask your client for one; it's for your use).

- Your name, address and tax no.

- Bank account no. or other payment method details. (You may prefer to put these on a separate PDF if the client is OK with that.)

- Date of issue. (And date of payment due?)

- Client's name, address and tax no.

- Service provided.

There is an example of a typical invoice on the next page.

John Brown (the translator/interpreter)

Tax no.: ABCDE12345

Address

INVOICE No.: 123 [For your own reference]

[+ client's invoice no. if they provide one.]

Date

CLIENT:
Client's name, business address and tax no.

Service/Project:

Job description & project no. (if the client/agency has one).	Fee	Word count / time	Amount due
Project 1. Translation of text about mushrooms ES>EN	€X /word	XX words	€XXX.XX
Project 2. Revision of text about pears ES>EN	€X /hour or word	XX minutes, hours or words	€XXX.XX
Total due			€XXX.XX

TOTAL:

(+ VAT etc. if applicable)

Total due = €XXX.XX

Payment details (bank account no., PayPal address etc.)

John Brown (Signed if necessary)

Payment due: (Date or "as of receipt of translated/revised text")

One of the simplest international payment methods is via an online payment service such as PayPal or Skrill. They are very simple to set up and use, though you must have at least a bank account to begin with. (Depending on your country or that of your client, there may by charges; check first.) They also have other services such as creation of invoices, handling tax etc. with templates. Mint.com is also useful for the latter if you are in the U.S.A. or Canada.

Good control over your finances is essential. You should have at the very least an Excel file listing your invoices sent, noting who has paid, how you found each client (or they found you) and any other useful information to give you an overview of how your business is going and where you think it should go. Investing in a finance and invoicing management system may save you a lot of time (and therefore money), e.g. www.4Visions.com, www.Gespoint.com or Translation Office 3000.

To check out new clients' financial reliability before agreeing to jobs, here are a few links:

- Companies House (Registry of companies in + 70 countries): http://ow.ly/nWol3001TGT

- World Payment Practices Free (Open forum for translators to ask about agencies etc.): https://groups.yahoo.com/neo/groups/WPPF/info

- As above in German: http://de.groups.yahoo.com/group/zahlungspraxis/

- Payment Practices (€20 / year):

    http://paymentpractices.net

- To check EU tax no.:

    http://ec.europa.eu/taxation_customs/vies/

- ProZ Blue Board:

    http://www.ProZ.com/blueboard

<u>Contracts: to sign or not to sign?</u>

Many direct clients will not require a contract to hire your services, though you may prefer to ask them for a purchase order anyhow. In any case, your email correspondence and confirmations may be enough to count as legally binding for such purposes.

Translation agencies, on the other hand, may ask you to fill in a Non-Disclosure Agreement, especially for sensitive legal texts, or a Contractor Agreement. These vary wildly in length and depth. You should have a good idea of what you are prepared to give and take before signing. They may include clauses dealing with matters you should consider such as:

- Your translation memories (TMs) and glossaries. (Do they belong to the agency?)

- Penalties for quality and deadlines.

- Copyright.

- Payment schedule, procedures and means.

- Liability.

- Non-compete clause.

The last two points are perhaps the most controversial, although all of these points may be used or abused. Make sure you are not liable for all damages due to mistakes in the translation, as this could lead to huge costs. The agency should proofread its texts well before delivery anyhow, and it is the agency who deals with the end client, not you. (Similarly, if the end client fails to pay, this is the agency's problem, not yours; check there are no abusive clauses in this respect.) Non-competition as far as an agency is concerned basically means you shouldn't take their clients from them. This is ethical common sense, but make sure there are no unreasonable or over-generalising clauses along the lines of: "the translator must not deal with the agency's future clients" etc., since you have no idea who their future clients will be. It is all very well to prevent unfair competition, but there is also such a thing as *fair* competition.

In any case, in my experience I have never had to refer to such contracts to solve problems since they usually just cover common sense and basic ethics that most of us will apply anyhow. Any doubts can usually be ironed out with a phone call. As I have said before, although unethical agencies may be big news, they are certainly not a representative majority. Fortunately, the vast majority of those working in the translation profession are decent, reasonable people. If there is a clause that you are very doubtful about, ask the agency to clarify it or don't sign. But in most cases, you really don't need to panic. Such contracts are common practice in some companies and countries.

And of course, the best way to avoid any liability claim or suchlike is to simply do good translations!

Mentors and partners

When starting out, you may find it wise to find a mentor, a translator with some years' experience about the day-to-day workings of freelance translation. You can find more experienced, successful fellow translators in translator forums or associations, for example. Simply ask for advice, explaining your situation. If they live in your area, they may even be prepared to chat with you in person from time to time, or let you shadow them as they work beside you. We can always learn a great deal from our colleagues.

They may even become a working partner one day, which can be useful for proofreading and reviewing each other's work, for example, or working on bigger projects.

Further reading

For much more advice on setting yourself up in freelance translation, there is the book by Oleg Rudavin: *Internet Freelancing: Practical Guide for Translators*, which is a good overview for beginners in the profession.

I would also recommend again David Allen's *Getting Things Done* for your freelance organisation, and Tim Ferriss' *4-Hour Work Week* with a plethora of advice for the digital entrepreneur and nomad.

Confessions

The idea behind the title of this book was inspired by Erik Hansson's now (in-)famous Facebook page *Things Translators Never Say* (TTNS), where translators come to tell of their experiences with weird and wonderful clients using more than a dash of humour. Below you'll find a host of situations that many translators will no doubt have experienced themselves. In a job where many work alone, the social networks have become extremely important not only for our work but to maintain our sanity and our sense of humour. I hope these little excerpts of mine from TTNS will help you to take your clients' foibles with a pinch of humour and see the lighter side of our sometimes stressful profession. Above all, remember to be patient with first-time clients who do not know what is required to do a good translation, and that "bad" clients such as those in the following pages are really a minority. ☺

The unreasonable client

If translators were chefs:

Customer: *"Hi! I need to book a table for twenty for my company's Christmas dinner in a couple of hours. Sorry we didn't book last month in November, but we've been very busy. Ah, we also don't have a big budget, so we're only interested in a cheap meal."*

Chef: *"Is it OK if I do it really cheaply for this evening but with sandwiches and the only table left next to the door?"*

Customer: *"No, of course not."*

Chef: *"Now I'm confused. OK, so tell me what meals you want me to cook and I'll let you know if it's possible in two hours."*

Customer: *"I'm afraid I can't tell you that before you confirm you can do the job."*

Chef: *"I see...so can you let me know if there are any vegetarians or people with allergies?"*

Customer: *"That's confidential information that I don't have anyway. So, how much will it cost? Can you prepare it for this evening?"*

Chef: *"What exactly do you want me to do...? Roast turkey? Greek salad?"*

Customer: *"You should know. You're the chef. Ah, and we'd like you to use our peculiar food, cutlery and pots and pans to cook with. I'll send you a hefty manual to teach you how to use them. You'll have to pay us to use them, of course. The food is mostly lettuce, but we'd like you to turn it into meat and dessert. And some water...for wine, of course. It's all a bit old and dirty, so you'll have to clean it up a bit, too."*

Chef: *"But the food may be off. The meal could be awful."*

Customer: *"That's not good enough. Our company expects a gourmet meal with amaretto truffles and tiramisu washed down with vintage Chianti. You'll have to improve the food when you work on it. By the way, we may change the order when you've started cooking. And more than twenty people may eventually turn up for dinner. Or fewer. Oh, and before we accept the meal, we'll be employing our own food taster, who has a bad cold. We also won't be able to pay you till March. And we'll need you to fill in these forms with your personal medical information and this contract admitting liability for possible stomach problems over the next ten years. So, see you in a couple of hours, OK? Hello? Hello...?"*

If translators were hairdressers:

Client:	*"Hello, I'd like a cheap, good-looking haircut right now, please*
Hairdresser:	*"All three...? OK, take a seat; I'll get to you after I've finished with this customer."*
Client:	*"Oh, I'm in a hurry. Here's an idea: give me the scissors while I'm waiting. I'll start trimming it myself, then you can 'clean it up' a bit, OK? And charge me less because I did some myself, of course."*

Client:	*"Could you tell us your fee and deadline for this project that you can't see?"*
Translator:	*"Yes, but first I need to know your sign of the Zodiac. Can you also scan your palm so my software can read it?"*

Translator:	*"okiwontchargeforpunctuationandspaces"*

Client:	"Can you give us a discount?"
Translator:	"Why?"
Client:	"..."

Client:	*"Can you translate this 25,000-word legal text for tomorrow?"*
Translator:	*"Are you at all concerned about quality?"*
Client:	*"No."*
Translator:	*"Then, yes, Google can; I mean I can."*

Dear client,

Thank you for sending me an audio file to transcribe. However, I will need some context. For example, why is the stuttering, lisping speaker apparently being gagged and strangled at the bottom of a swimming pool five hundred yards away from the microphone?

Dear translator,

We have a finely crafted, superb text to be translated within the next five days. To do so, we've sent it to our 17-year-old trainee for four days and now you have one day to hurriedly proofread it. Please find regurgitated dog's dinner attached.

Client:	"I know translators prepared to charge less."
Translator:	"I know clients prepared to pay more."

Client: *"Can you translate a text?"*

Translator: *"That's what I do. Is it the Encyclopaedia Britannica or a recipe for pancakes?"*

Client: *"It's quite technical. Lots of graphs and diagrams."*

Translator: *"May I see said graphs and diagrams?"*

Client: *"No. I think it would be far more efficient for me to describe them to you over the phone in painstaking detail for the next twenty minutes without pausing for breath, just like the sentences I write, which as you may have noticed go on and on and on and—"*

Translator: *"I see your colleague has already sent it in PDF format. Can you send it in Word so I can work on it more easily?"*

Client: *"Afraid not. I feel it would be more productive to make the job as difficult as possible so that you really make an effort. Oops, did I say that out loud...?"*

Translator: *"Just found the Word version by searching for 'doc' on your website. But I don't see the graphs or diagrams."*

Client: *"Oh, no, I haven't drawn them yet. They're still in my head. Can you read my mind with your magic software?"*

Client:	*"I speak English quite well but I've got a text with lots of complicated words. I can translate it, then you can revise it, OK?"*
Translator:	*"When you say the text has 'lots of complicated words', do you mean you can't actually translate it?"*
Client:	*"Of course I can translate it. I just don't understand the words."*
Translator:	*"Umm...isn't that the same thing?"*
Client:	*"I understand words like 'and', 'but' and 'the'. I just don't get the bits in between."*
Translator:	*"By 'bits in between' do you mean almost the entire text...?"*
Client:	*"Well, there are lots of easy words like "of" and "it". I don't see why I should pay you to translate them. Look, if you're going to be picky, I could spend all week taking out all the words like 'in', 'do' and 'to', but then I won't know where to put them back. So you'll have to tell me."*
Translator:	*"Can you tell me what you think the difference is between 'translation' and 'revision'?*
Client:	*"Oooh, about 15 cents a word. Hello...?"*

If translators were car mechanics:

Client: *"Can you repair my car? I need it for tomorrow."*

Translator: *"Can I see it?"*

Client: *"No. Not until you tell me if you can fix it."*

Translator: *"Um...What kind of car is it?"*

Client: *"A blue one."*

Translator: *"I mean the manufacturer and model."*

Client: *"That's personal information I don't want to disclose. When will it be ready?"*

Translator: *"Well...what noises has it been making? How old? Mileage?"*

Client: *"Questions, questions! Am I supposed to tell you how to do your job? Just tell me how long it'll take to fix it. Oh, and I can only afford €X. And I want you to use these complicated, old, rusty tools of mine. I've also started to tinker with the car myself, so you should give me a discount now you only have to finish off the job. And fix that leak I made while tinkering. Here's a blurry photo of it to help."*

Translator: *"Hmm...It looks like a Trabant from the Soviet bloc period. Do you have the manufacturer's manual to give me a general idea?*

Client: *"Yes, here you are."*

Translator: *"This manual is for a Mini."*

Client: *"Mini, Trabant...they're both cars, right? Anyway, it doesn't matter because I want it to be a Rolls Royce when you've finished. A red one. I know a mechanic down the street who says he can do that for five euros in half an hour. I'd do it myself but I don't have the time because I have a proper job. I can drive, so I know a lot about cars."*

Translator: *"Actually, they don't make these car parts anymore. Maybe I can send for them from Cuba."*

Client: *"Whatever. Just make sure it's ready tomorrow so my cousin can take it for a test drive with his myopia and arthritis after a few drinks in the pub. If he's satisfied with the drive, we may have more jobs for you in the next decade. By the way, in order to pay you, I'll need a complete list and sworn, stamped copies of all your diplomas, training courses and previous employers with their addresses, phone numbers and blood groups. Just send them by express post to our head office in Bhutan before tomorrow. Bye, then. See you next year—er, I mean tomorrow...though I might call you today every five minutes to see how you're doing, tell you how to do your job and maybe just whine and send someone to poke you with a stick occasionally to encourage you with such managerial skills, as this will surely help you work faster and better. I might also change my requests and give you additional little jobs like changing the tyres, fitting a new radio etc. once you've started. At no extra cost. What do you mean, 'no'? How unprofessional of you to refuse work. Somebody will do it..."*

Translator:

Would you like the style of the text to be upbeat and lively, or sombre and serious?

Client:

We're not sure. We'll tell you when we see the translation in a language we don't understand.

[Translator sighs heavily and does the translation in a sombre, serious style.]

Client:

The text seems too sombre and serious. Can you make it more upbeat and lively?

[Translator sends the same text with colourful fonts.]

Client:

Perfect!

Turning the tables

Client:	*"Have you finished the translation?"*
Translator:	*"Yes. Please fill in this NDA and liability waiver before I can send my work to you, as I did when you sent me the source text."*
Client:	*"Oh... Done. Can we have it now?"*
Translator:	*"Of course. Please go to my automated system and fill in the client questionnaire, similar to your own."*
Client:	*"Hmm...Done at last. Please send the translation."*
Translator:	*"Here it is. Please find the badly scanned document attached, matching the source text's format."*
Client:	*"Don't you have it in Word?"*
Translator:	*"Of course...with the usual surcharge."*

Dear agency,

What a coincidence that you're expanding your database of translators.

I too am expanding my database of agencies. With that in mind, I would also like you to do a free test proofreading for me. Please find the medical and legal texts attached. I will need them by next Monday morning, SOB. (I am afraid that I will be unavailable after beer p.m. today.)

So that I may also test your payment services, you can also find my PayPal information attached. Let's see how quickly and efficiently you can send me €XXX.

If am satisfied, you can do it all again for me next weekend. ☺

P.S. I am attaching a form for you to explain why I should work with you, since I didn't find any such information in your email.

Time wasters

Client: *"Hello. How is the translation going?"*

Translator: *"Quite slowly, I'm afraid. I keep getting phone calls and emails from somebody interrupting me."*

Client: *"Oh. So why don't you tell them you're busy?"*

Translator: *"OK. I'm busy."* CLICK.

Client: *"Can you translate a text with software X?"*

Translator: *"Sorry, I use software Y and software Z."*

Client: *"I've heard software Z can convert software X."*

Translator: *"Maybe. Send me the text and I'll tell you."*

Client: *"If it can, how many words can you do this week?"*

Translator: *"Send me the text and I'll tell you."*

Client: *"It's not complicated. Do you think you'll need pictures?"*

Translator:	*"Send me the text and I'll tell you."*
Client:	*"Do you have experience in this kind of text?"*
Translator:	*"Send me the text and I'll tell you."*
Client:	*"Shall I send you the text so you can tell me?"*
Translator:	*"No. Please go away."*

Client:	*"I'll translate this 10,000-word urgent text roughly this morning and you can clean it up this afternoon. I'll pay you € X for that."*
Translator:	*"What happens if your translated text is incomprehensible?"*
Client:	*"Then you can tell me the bits you don't understand and I'll write them in my native language for you to translate those parts."*
Translator:	*"And if it's all completely incomprehensible?"*
Client:	*"Then I can rewrite it all in my language and you can translate it all. This evening. For the same fee."*
Translator:	*"You have distracted me from playing Candy Crush for two minutes. Go away."*

Always urgent

Client:	*"We have a huge rush project to be handed in next month. We need you to be available 24/7."*
Translator:	*"Unfortunately, lack of food and sleep causes death within days, so I won't be able to meet that deadline. Are you based in North Korea?"*

Client:	*"We can't accept your urgent fee. Can you do it more cheaply?"*
Translator:	*"Sure. Here's my normal fee."*
Client:	*"Great! Can you do it today? It's urgent."*

Dear client,

Thank you for asking about my availability. Unfortunately, I have just checked my calendar and discovered that between Friday and Monday there is a weekend.

Client:	*Urgent job for today. Can you do it?*
Translator:	*Sorry. Not available.*
Client:	*I understand. Here it is. For 5 p.m. please.*
Translator:	*Did you actually read my mail?*
Client:	*Yes. I understand. There'll be more tomorrow.*
Translator:	*Have you just been on one of those hardline sales courses that teach you how to passively-aggressively ignore everyone's opinions and feelings?*
Client:	*Yes! How did you know?*
Translator:	*I understand.*

Client:	*Hello. We need this text translated in the next hour!*
Translator:	*Well, that's a very tight deadline. My fee will be €X.*
Client:	*Hmm…I'll have to think about that. I'll get back to you in an hour or two.*

The linguistically challenged client

A long-winded, unintelligible sentence with no commas...

Translator's comment:

"Perhaps there are some commas missing which could greatly clarify this sentence?"

Client's reply:

"Yes."

An advertising slogan is born:

Translator:

"Dear client,

I have some questions regarding the advertising campaign slogan for your fast food chain: "its kool for kidz". Is the crazy spelling and punctuation based on a target social group of underprivileged children? Could I see the market research upon which you based the slogan? Or at least if you could tell me about its anthropological and psychological basis, I will be in a better position to produce a slogan for a similar intended audience and effect in the target country and culture."

Client:

"what you meen crazy speling and puntuation? whats rong with the slogen? weve alredy printed the flyers and got a tv campain redy and all that and stuff so we cant change it now anyway. just translate it. it looks all rite to me.

in fact, "i'm lovin it".

Helo. Were looking 4 a proofreeder. Helo...?

"Dear client:

I understand that the translation is needed urgently (again), but if you take five minutes longer on writing the source text and use whole words instead of abbrev.s, you'll find that the prcss wll go mch fster bcs I cn undrstd & no ask u ev 10 secs WTF u mean. SOB."

| Client: | *"When will computers be able to translate as well as humans?"* |
| Translator: | *"When they can write* Macbeth.*"* |

Client:	*"My level of English is poor, so can you translate this cover letter into flawless English? It's for an important job post for which I'll have to speak and write fluent English, so it has to be word perfect."*
Translator:	*"Okayyyyy...but when you get the job or go to the interview, I foresee a little problem..."*

Dear Client,

You may wish to revise your use of punctuation, particularly the colon:

"The key to our company's success: lies in our corporate philosophy."

Dear client,

Your text is riddled with mistakes and barely intelligible. Please write it again in your native language and let me translate it.

Dear translator,

The texts alredy in our langwage were english.

Client: *Please proofread this text so we can publish it. Thanks.*

Translator: *Please note that the structure of the text is fundamentally flawed, with circular arguments and repeated points. It is also rather verbose and jumps suddenly between matters with no apparent connection.*

               I would advise you to write it well in your native language first, then let me translate it.

Client: *Just correct the text.*

One month later:

Client: *We have received this review from the publisher. Please apply the necessary changes:*

               "The text is fundamentally flawed, with circular arguments and repeated points. It is also rather verbose and jumps suddenly between matters with no apparent connection."

Translator: *I am afraid I won't be available today. I have to go to hospital to get some splinters from my desk removed from my forehead.*

Client: *I hear that translators these days use software and build up a "translation memory" and glossary for particular clients. Is that true? Would you do that with us?*

Translator: *Yes, it's true; but I'm afraid it won't work with your particular texts. It only works with texts whose words are spelled the same way more than once.*

Client's text: *"This year we are going to develop a completely new plan. It is a plan we developed last year."*

Translator: *Do you mean "This year we are going to* carry out *a new plan that we* prepared *last year"?*

Client: *Yes, but we prefer "develop". Always. It's lovely. Just develop the text like that and develop the invoice so our accounts department can develop it.*

Client's text: *By reducing the time, queues are reduced, giving a reduction in complaints.*

Translator: *"Perhaps you could use a thesaurus to find a greater variety of words?"*

Client's text 2: *By plummeting the temporal duration, the amount of population waiting in orderly lines is downgraded, rendering a discount in whingeing.*

Dear client,

Please find the translated text attached, full of hackneyed clichés, mixed metaphors, redundancies, circular arguments, erroneous information, misspellings, plagiarism and culturally offensive remarks. As instructed, the translation faithfully reflects the original. Please find my invoice attached.

Client:

"Your translation doesn't look at all like the original text!

It doesn't have all those capital letters for words We Think are Important. And our gigantic sentences beginning with "And" have been divided up with full stops and commas. And it doesn't have lots of repeated exclamation marks like this!!!!!"

Translator: Do you need the text in US American English?

Client: No British.

Translator: OK, no British. But what about American?

Dear translator,

I could not help but notice that, upon reading your translated version of my original text, you appear to have utilized far fewer words than was my case upon drafting the text which you worked upon in order to produce said translation, resulting, inevitably, in a much shorter translated version than the original version, and leading me to wonder what criteria made you decide to produce the former concise version in preference over the latter wordier text and if you would be so good as to provide me with an explanation for said apparent shift in style since, as you may have perceived on reading this sentence, I am rather fond of sentences that are impossible to pronounce without drawing several breaths and losing the thread, perhaps because I believe that this makes me sound more intelligent and erudite when in fact it just makes me more boring and unintelligible, for example when I use several superfluous, excess synonyms and words that mean the same thing just to fill up space because I was asked to write a text with a certain amount of words, for example the two hundred words used to create this meandering, long-winded, oversized, lengthy sentence.

Translator:

If I earned a dollar for every lack of concordance in this text, I'll have a million euros by yesterday.

Cheapskates

Agency: *"If we are satisfied with your work, there could be more."*

Translator: *"If I were satisfied with your fee, I would bother to reply."*

Agency: *"Our end client pays us after 90 days."*

Translator: *"And what has that got to do with me?"*

Agency: *"We only pay for target text words."*

Translator: *"I'm feeling very verbose today..."*

Translator:

"My basic fee for proofreading English is $X.

My basic fee for translating from Spanish is $3X.

My basic fee for translating to and from your Spanglish is $100X. (Please don't attempt the translation yourself.)"

Template for bottom-feeders and slave-drivers:

Dear [job title or misspelled name],

I hope this mail finds you [incongruous adjective or adverb]. We are pleased/proud to offer you [our services/the opportunity to work] [wrong preposition] [job description].

Our rates start at [ridiculous number] and we offer translations in [long list of languages copied and pasted from Wikipedia, including Sioux, Cornish and Khoisan click languages].

We specialise in [list copied and pasted from a university prospectus, including thirteenth century Japanese architecture, quantum mechanics, Mayan astrology and dialectical idealism].

We are Highly Professional [so much so that we use capital letters to emphasise it] and [list of bland, overused corporate adjectives (e.g. passionate, pro-active, a leader, etc.)].

Our [job title]s are qualified natives with much experience [but for some reason they didn't help write this email].

Looking to hear of you soon [or similarly incorrect phrase]!!! [Random amount of exclamation marks]

[Hotmail, Yahoo or Bhutanese URL]

[Logo of ostrich, umbrella or other incongruous image unrelated to languages]

[Forgotten automatic footnotes that have not been deleted, including company department where the author actually works in a cubicle, invitations to online casinos generated by their resident virus, and links to personal social network pages with snaps taken on holiday, drinking beers in pyjamas with pet dog, etc.]

Translator: *Here's my proofreading fee.*

Client: *You don't have to check people's names etc., so you could take out those words from the fee.*

Translator: *What if I told you that three people's names are misspelled in the first paragraph?*

Client: *Which ones?*

Translator: *Here's my fee again.*

Client: "Can you translate an instructions manual?"

Translator: "Depends. Is it about how to use a spoon or how to build a space shuttle?"

Client: "Can't tell you yet. 5,000 words."

Translator: "Well, my minimum fee is €X/word."

Client: "Ouch. We can only do half that."

Translator: "Shall I do half the translation?"

Client: "Do you know any other translators?"

Translator: "Lots."

Client: "Great!"

Translator: "They charge the same as me."

Client: "That's not very helpful."

Translator: "When I go to a shop, I don't usually ask the shopkeeper if they know another shop where I can buy the same products for half the price. That would be…hmm…what's the word…?"

Client: "*BEEP…BEEP…BEEP*"

Translator: "…Daft?"

Client: *Could you translate these 30,000 words for tomorrow? Well, some are in our language and some are in English. Just translate the bits in Spanish and proofread the bits in English.*

Translator: *Why don't you write it all in one language?*

Client: *Because that would take a really long time! That would be impossible before tomorrow.*

Translator: *You don't say. Like translating and proofreading it, you mean?*

Client: *Umm...*

Client: "If you accept this job, we can give you much more in future."

Translator: "Money?"

Client: "Work."

Translator: *"Click. Beep. Beep. Beep."*

The oddball editor

Client:

"Hello.

We have an urgent text to translate. Please find it attached. We only need the yellow bits translated. The blue bits need proofreading. The green bits are for context. The pink bits look nice. Please hurry."

Translator:

"Dear anonymous, hysterical editor,

While the adjective "urgent" is becoming superfluous in emails from your company, I would appreciate knowing who is writing to me—animal, mineral or vegetable? The only thing I know is that, according to a previous email, your company "specialises in communication", though emails such as the one you have just sent clearly belie this.

A quick look at the text immediately leads me to redefine your colour code:

Yellow: The difficult bits you realized you couldn't do after accepting the job now that there are only 12 hours left before the deadline, after doing all the "easy bits", including half-sentences.

Blue: The "fairly easy bits" you're not entirely sure have been properly translated by your seventeen-year-old intern on parole, who rattled them off in his coffee break.

Green: The bits that are essential to read in order to understand the text but which you don't intend to pay for.

Pink: The bits your graphic designer has meddled with, taking out unsightly commas, accents, etc., correction of which you don't intend to pay for either.

Whilst I would be delighted to help you out, if only for the sake of your long-suffering end clients, I feel my time would be more usefully employed for humanity and enjoyably for myself by spending all day staring at the ceiling, for example."

"Dear Translator,
Could you simply translate these few strings we forgot to put in the text last year? I don't remember where they go or any context. Thanks."

- Get
- Of
- X
- Do
- P.C.
- To
- Danger! Risk of death! Read instructions much careful no mistaking: Do not «INSERT STRING» while operating «INSERT STRING». Report any «INSERT STRING» to the «INSERT STRING» immediately.

Client: *"To simplify this technical text, we've taken out all the pictures and reference material."*

Translator: *"Gee, thanks. That'll help."* (Head-to-desk.)

Client:

"'The Earth is twice the size of Jupiter and its atmosphere is mostly helium.'

Where is the mistake? It looks like perfect English to us."

Client: *Could you possibly get round to making a shorter version of this text?*

Translator: *Do you mean if I can summarise it?*

Client: *That is affirmative. The text is written below these lines:*

                      "In the month of September of the year 2012, the broadcaster BBC broadcast the film Star Wars..."

Translator: *Do you think your readers are aware that September is a month, 2012 is a year, the BBC is a broadcaster (see the initials) and that Star Wars is a film?*

Client: *That may be a possible. Why?*

Client: "Please revise the bits of text in blue. The main text in black is OK, so we don't need to pay for that."

Translator: "OK, so delete the black text and just send me the blue text."

Client: "But the blue texts makes no sense without the black text. You need the black text to understand the blue text. Ah."

[Sound of penny dropping.]

Client: "My nephew's very good at English. He took a look at your text and made a few comments. Please make any necessary changes."

Translator: "Is he pretty good at maths, too? Maybe he could check your company's yearly accounts."

Client: "What? That would be really stupid! Oh…"

The dodgy contract

Non-disclosure contract small print:

"Clause 2876 B, Sub-Section F, Point iv: Should the translator or any vaguely related person work with any of our clients or our clients' clients or our clients' clients' clients at any time within two centuries prior to or after signing this contract, either with or without said translator's knowledge (or that of family members, friends, acquaintances, contacts, spammers or passers-by in the street), or reply to any of said parties' emails, or mention them in a forum, or read about them or overhear their name in a conversation about any topic however trivially related or unrelated anywhere on Earth, even in their sleep, they shall be required to endure the ever-burning lakes of hell for a period of no fewer than twenty generations of their offspring.* *Applicable whether or not this contract has been read, understood, signed, received in spam folder or eaten by pet dog, cat or other sentient or non-sentient being, dead or alive."

The doomed translator

"Helo, i hav a reelly urgent job offer but its so urgently that i dont having 1 minute to write proper to a forum of profesinally text writers. Insted, ill take 10 seconnds to destroying my reputation and carrer in front off thosands oof my colleegs for the rest of my liffe. That will be very more intelligently. Plees writting return soon. Kises."

The insistent client

Translator: *"When you say* commercialise, *do you simply mean 'sell', or do you mean 'market', 'negotiate', 'trade', 'advertise', 'put on the market', 'brand', 'launch the product', 'make it profitable', 'exploit it', 'turn it into a business'...?"*

Client: "Commercialise *means all those things. And* 'sell'."

Translator: *"So you mean all those things when you say* 'We are going to commercialise X'...?"

Client: *"No. We just mean 'sell' in this case. But we prefer the term* 'commercialise'. *It sounds more professional."*

Translator: *"And you're sure that your end client understands that you mean 'sell' when you say 'commercialise', so that there's no possible confusion?"*

Client: *"Of course. Everyone knows that 'commercialise' means 'sell'. But we prefer 'commercialise'."*

313

Translator: *"But you do actually want to sell your product to your end client...?"*

Client: *"Of course we want to sell it. I mean commercialise it. But just put 'commercialise'."*

Two hours after delivering the translation:

Client: *"Please translate this email from our end client."*

End client's email:

"Do you intend to sell us your product?"

Translator: *"I would advise you to say 'the EU' instead of 'Europe'."*

Client: *"Just translate."*

Text: *"We export to countries outside Europe such as Switzerland."*

The dodgy source text

Translator:

"Dear international magazine editor,
  Your texts sound like they have been translated by Google."

Client:

"Dear translator,
Thanks! I translated them myself!"

[Not a hint of irony. Translator silently begins to plot editor's grisly "accident".]

Dear client,

I am writing to warn you that your source texts about important government bodies are wildly inaccurate and full of dreadful grammatical errors.

Oh, wait a moment; I see you have simply copied them directly from the government's official websites...

Dear lawyer,

I am sorry to hear that you are incapable of transcribing or clearly photocopying the legal document, which you unfortunately seem to have written on used toilet paper, then photocopied on a rusty machine in need of a good dusting. Please find the translation attached.

Translation:

On [illegible date], Mr [illegible] is hereby ordered to [illegible] on pain of death. If he does not [illegible], then he shall be obliged to pay the sum of [illegible] to [illegible] for [illegible] unless [illegible].

I, [large stamp blotting out name], hereby attest to [handwritten text seemingly written by a chimpanzee with arthritis] on the following date: [coffee or wine stain].

[Possibly a signature or an ink blot.]

Please find my crystal clear invoice attached.

When the translator is not a translator

Client: *"We need a translation today."*

Translator: *"I see. Could you please tell me: the context, style, how long is it (an internal memo or the* Complete Works of Shakespeare *(several harrowing tragedies spring to mind when I work with you…)), the context, the format and the target audience? Perhaps I could take a look? Thanks."*

Client: *"You know the context. It's all about that contract you translated last month."*

Translator: *"Fine. And the style?"*

Client: *"Oh, quite casual, nothing formal."*

Translator: *"OK. We're getting there. Perhaps in your next email you could tell me who the intended audience of the translation is?"*

Client: *"That company that wants to sue us."*

Translator: *"As I suspected…Format?"*

Client: *"What do you mean 'format'? I just told you: 'casual'."*

Translator (scratching head):

                   "Could I actually set my eyes on the task in question, perhaps?"

Client:	*"Sure, as I said, today. Could you at least tell us if you can do it today?"*
Translator:	*"That depends. How long is it?"*
Client:	*"Oh, about two hours, I should think. If you can't manage that today, how about on Friday?"*
Translator:	*"Do you mean 'by' Friday? Maybe I can start today."*
Client:	*"We mean 'on' Friday. That's when we're meeting our English client again."*
Translator:	*"Ah. I see you mean 'interpreter', not 'translator'. Excuse me a moment while I smash my head against the desk."*

The over-zealous proofreader

Client: *"Our proofreader has changed all of the idioms and proverbs you translated!"*

Translator: *May I see the changes?"*

Client: *"Here they are:*

'The precipitation is in the form of canines and felines.'

'A feathered friend in the fist is of more value than twice the number in the shrub.'

'Don't enumerate your fowl prior to the newborn appearing from the ova.'

Translator: *"Well, you know what they say: 'One isn't able to train an aged canine in modern skills.'"*

Etiquette for translators

A tip for translators when asked the following inevitable questions at events unrelated to translation:

"Translator? Can you live off that?"

"Translator? Doesn't Google do that?"

"Translator? My nephew speaks that language pretty well. Shall I give you his number?"

"Translator? How many languages do you speak?"

"Translator? I saw a video all about this bit of plastic you stick in your ear that enables you to chat up attractive people all over the world with a voice like Stephen Hawking and The Terminator. Apparently it's coming out next week. Though they've been saying that every week since the Beta version was released, which I think was in the first episode of Star Trek. Correct me if I'm wrong. Do you speak Klingon?"

"Translator? I do a bit of that. Perhaps you'd like to translate my company's marketing campaign and yearly accounts? I'd do it myself, but I don't have time because I have a proper job. I'll buy you a beer. And peanuts."

"Translator? Don't you get confused speaking two languages at the same time? Do you know any politicians?"

Tip:

Always keep both hands occupied, for example with a coffee and a canapé. This will prevent you from reflexively hitting your interlocutor.

The Luddite

Client:
"We need this translation this very afternoon, but we don't want you to use that 'Computer Aided Translation' software we've vaguely heard about. It sounds suspicious."

Translator:
"Of course. Please copy the text by hand and send it by horse and carriage or bring it to my office on foot from your country. I don't trust this new-fangled 'electronic mail'.

P.S. This message contains no virus other than my sneezing on the parchment on which it is written.

Basic Translator's Glossary

Alignment: Aligning an entire text with its previous translation for comparison, etc.

Back Translation: Translating a translation back into the source language.

Bitext: The same text in two different languages placed side by side for comparison, study, etc.

CAT tool: Computer Aided Translation tool.

Consistency: The extent to which a term is used to translate the same source term in the same way and in the same context throughout a text.

Corpus: A large, structured body of texts in which to find typical terminology in a specific field, period, country, profession, company, etc.

Concordance: Suitability of a word or expression in a given context, found by comparing its different uses, for example in previously translated texts from the same client or field.

DTP: Desktop Publishing.

EOB: End Of Business (time of day).

Fuzzy match:	A partial match with a term in your TM.
LSP:	Language Service Provider.
LV:	Language Vendor.
MT:	Machine Translation.
NDA:	Non-Disclosure Agreement (contract).
PM:	Project Manager.
PO:	Purchase Order (confirmation of job allocation and payment conditions etc.).
Post-editing:	Editing and reviewing by humans after machine translation (not recommended!).
QA:	Quality Assurance (LQA = Language QA, FQA = Formatting QA, etc.).
Reverse Translation:	Translation of a text by a mother-tongue speaker into a foreign language. (This is not standard practice.)
SLA:	Service Level Agreement (contract).
SOB:	Start of Business (and something else you may say if it's very early…)

Source text:	The original text in the original language.
SOW:	Statement of Work (contract).
Target text:	The final text in the translated language.
TEP:	Translation, Editing and Proofreading.
Termbase:	Database of terminology and related information, usually multilingual.
TM:	Translation Memory.
TMX:	Translation Memory Exchange. Widely used format to convert, export and import TMs.
Transcription:	Writing down oral language (e.g. speech in a video).
TU:	Translation Unit (a section of text then committed to the TM on completion).

About the author

Gary Smith is an experienced freelance translator. He has given webinars and talks at many translation congresses internationally and around Spain and was the president of the Valencia region's association of translators and interpreters, La Xarxa (www.xarxativ.es). Today he represents IAPTI in Spain. He has also published articles in the American Translators Association's monthly magazine, *The Chronicle*, and other reputable online media.

@GaryGlokalize

www.ingramcontent.com/pod-product-compliance
Lightning Source LLC
Chambersburg PA
CBHW060541200326
41521CB00007B/443